COMPACT
Aktives Lernen

UNREGELMÄSSIGE VERBEN ENGLISCH

schnell kapiert

Ute Elfers

Compact Verlag

© 2000 Compact Verlag München

Alle Rechte vorbehalten. Nachdruck, auch auszugsweise, nur mit ausdrücklicher Genehmigung des Verlages gestattet.

Chefredaktion: Ilse Hell
Redaktion: Karina Partsch, Manuela Schomann
Redaktionsassistenz: Katharina Eska, Stefanie Sommer
Produktionsleitung: Gunther Jaich
Umschlaggestaltung: Inga Koch
ISBN 3-8174-7159-9
7371591

Besuchen Sie uns im Internet: wwww.compactverlag.de

Inhalt

Vorwort 4

Unregelmäßige Verben 5

Lösungen zu den Übungen 111

Anhang 127

Vorwort

Der korrekte Gebrauch der unregelmäßigen Verben in der englischen Sprache bereitet dem Lernenden oft Schwierigkeiten. Im Englischen ist es aber unerlässlich diese richtig anzuwenden, da gerade die unregelmäßigen Verben zu den am häufigsten gebrauchten Verben der Sprache zählen.

In diesem Buch wird der Lernende nicht nur systematisch mit der Bildung der wichtigsten unregelmäßigen Verben vertraut gemacht, sondern er erhält zudem einen Überblick über die unterschiedlichsten Verwendungskontexte der einzelnen Verben.

Zu jedem Verb werden die Stammformen und Grundbedeutungen angegeben, die anhand von Beispielsätzen verdeutlicht werden. Im Anschluss an die Beispielsätze folgen verschiedene Redewendungen, die mit dem jeweiligen Verb gebildet werden können.

Durch Übersetzungsübungen vom Englischen ins Deutsche werden weitere Bedeutungen eines Verbs eingeführt und deren Gebrauch trainiert und vertieft. Die Lösungen zu den Übungen befinden sich am Ende des Buchs.

Das Buch orientiert sich primär am britischen Sprachgebrauch (BE). Unter „Beachte" sind vor allem Unterschiede zum amerikanischen Englisch (AE) und zum Deutschen genannt. Die Hinweise geben nützliche Zusatzinformationen, die mit dem Verb zusammenhängen.

Im Anhang sind zur Vervollständigung weitere unregelmäßige Verben des Englischen aufgeführt, die heute aber eher ungebräuchlich sind.

„Unregelmäßige Verben Englisch – schnell kapiert" eignet sich sowohl zum Nachschlagen als auch zum systematischen Lernen und Einüben.

Unregelmäßige Verben

awake awoke/awaked
awoken/awaked *aufwachen; wecken*

I always awake at the same time in the morning.
Suddenly a loud noise awoke me.
This photo has awoken memories in the past.

◄ Idioms

to awake to something – *sich einer Sache bewusst werden*
to awake someone to something – *jemandem etwas zum Bewusstsein bringen*
to awake to the joys of something – *plötzlich Vergnügen an etwas finden*

◄ Übung

His silly remark awoke/awaked her anger.
The child awoke crying from a nightmare.

◄ Beachte

Es gibt auch das regelmäßig gebildete Verb "to awaken": z.B. The customer's behaviour awakened her anger.
Wie "awake" wird gebildet:
wake woke/waked woken/waked – *aufwachen; wecken*

be was/were been *sein*

Lovely weather, isn't it?
I used to be a very good athlete when I was young.
When we arrived, the police had already been there.

◄ Idioms

that is the be all and end all – *das ist das A und O*
to be about to do something – *im Begriff sein, etwas zu tun*
to be all ears – *ganz Ohr sein*
to be in one's right mind – *bei vollem Verstand sein*
to be in the know – *eingeweiht sein*
to be in the picture – *im Bilde, informiert sein*
to be on the safe side,... – *um ganz sicher zu gehen,...*
to be off the hook – *aus dem Schneider sein*
to be out of date – *altmodisch sein*
to be out of sorts – *nicht auf der Höhe sein, sich nicht so gut fühlen*
to be at ease – *sich wohl bzw. wie zu Hause fühlen*
be that as it may – *sei es wie es wolle, trotzdem*

Übung

Visitors are able to leave the exhibition at 5 o'clock.
For the time being we must try to do without his help.
Don't wear this coat! It's out of fashion.

bear   bore   borne (born)   *tragen, ertragen; gebären*

The boss of this company bears a heavy responsibility.
I wondered who the letter was from because it bore no signature.
She bore the loss of her husband with dignity.
My mother has born seven children.
I was born in Massachusetts.

Idioms

to bear something in mind – *etwas nicht vergessen, an etwas denken*
to bear resemblance to – *Ähnlichkeit haben mit*
to bear up – *durchhalten, standhalten*
to bear someone down – *zu Boden drücken, überwältigen*
to bear arms against someone – Krieg führen gegen jemanden
to bear away – *mitnehmen*
to bear examination – *einer Prüfung standhalten*
to bear north – *sich nach Norden halten*
to bear off – *abdrehen*
to be borne along – *mitgetragen werden*
to bring pressure to bear on somebody – *Druck auf jemanden ausüben*

Übung

I cannot bear him. He is such a nasty person.
You will have to bear the consequence when things go wrong.
We will certainly bear all costs involved.
My failure bore very hard on me for a long time.

beat   beat   beaten   *schlagen*

Beat two eggs, then add sugar and flour.
My friend always beats me at tennis.
The children were beaten every day.

That beats everything! – *Das ist doch die Höhe!*
Can you beat it! – *Das darf doch nicht wahr sein!*

to beat about the bush – *um die Sache herumreden*
to beat a retreat – *das Feld räumen, klein beigeben*
to beat something into someone – *jemandem etwas einbläuen*
to beat the deadline – *die Frist einhalten*
to beat a path to somebody's door – *jemandem die Bude einrennen*
to beat the air – *herumfuchteln*
Beat it! – *Hau ab! Verschwinde!*
to beat somebody into second place – *jemanden auf den zweiten Platz verweisen*
I'm beaten! – *Ich gebe mich geschlagen!*

Last night we were beaten up by a gang of hooligans.
Finally the fire-brigade beat back the fire.
The waves were beating against the shore.
What do you want here? Beat it!

become became become   *werden*

I hope I will become a famous actor one day.
She became very angry when she found out that he had been lying to her.
It has become a general habit to go shopping on Thursday nights.

to become the rule – *zur Regel werden*
to become interested in somebody – *anfangen, sich für jemanden zu interessieren*
to become king – *König werden*

We have not seen him for ages. Do you know what has become of him?
What's to become of her? She can't stay with us.
Your new colleague is becoming a problem.

"become" bedeutet nicht dt. *„bekommen"*

begin began begun   *anfangen*

If you are ready, we can begin.
The film begins with a murder.

Shortly after midnight it began to rain.
The lecture always began at ten o'clock in the morning.
When she saw me, she began to laugh.
I have begun to count the days until his arrival.
I should have begun collecting material for my paper long ago.
The concert had already begun when she rushed on the stage.
As the rain did not stop, she began to tell them a story.
Say your names beginning from the back.
To begin with there were only five.

Idioms

to begin with,... – *erstens, zunächst einmal...*
well begun is half done – *gut begonnen ist halb gewonnen*
to begin on something – *etwas in Angriff nehmen*
to begin an attack – *zum Angriff schreiten*
to begin school – *eingeschult werden*
to begin a rumour – *ein Gerücht in die Welt setzen*
to begin in business – *ein Geschäft aufmachen*
beginning from Monday – *von Montag an*
beginning from page 20 – *von Seite 20 an*
since the world began – *seit Anbeginn der Welt*
that doesn't even begin to compare with ... – *das lässt sich nicht mal annähernd mit ... vergleichen*
I can't begin to thank you for what you've done. – *Ich kann Ihnen gar nicht genug dafür danken, was Sie getan haben.*
to begin by saying that ... – *einleitend sagen, dass ...*
where the hair begins – *am Haaransatz*

Übung

When did you begin learning English?
He is planning to go on a trip to Alaska. For this reason he has begun to save up all his money.
My grandfather began as a factory worker and became manager later in life.
I am looking for a word beginning with X.
I had just begun my book when the telephone rang.
She'll begin the new job next month.
The child began to feel tired.
He's beginning to understand.
Their mother begun to fear the worst when the telephone rang.
The trouble began when he came back from Russia.
She tried to take her revenge by beginning a rumour about him.

bend   bent   bent   *biegen; beugen*

He always bends over the table when he eats.
This metal bends easily.
Since I had the accident, I cannot bend my back.
Her head was bent over her book.
He bent the iron bar as if it were a piece of wire.

to bend one's energies on something – *seine ganze Kraft auf etwas verwenden*
to bend one's knee – *sich unterwerfen*
on bended knees – *auf Knien*
to bend oneself to a task – *sich einer Aufgabe widmen*
to bend out of shape – *verbiegen*
to bend over backwards to do something – *sich übermäßig anstrengen, sich sehr bemühen, etwas zu tun*
to bend the rules – *die Regeln etwas lockern*
to bend someone to one's will – *sich jemanden gefügig machen*
to be bent on doing something – *entschlossen, erpicht sein, etwas zu tun*
to bend something at right angles – *etwas rechtwinklig abbiegen*
to bend the law – *das Gesetz beugen*

◄ Idioms

In this valley the river bends many times.
She bent down to pick up a piece of paper.
You should bend your mind to your studies.
Do not bend the pages of your new book!
The bumper got bent in the crash.
My leg won't bend.

◄ Übung

bet   bet/betted   bet/betted   *wetten*

I bet that it will snow tomorrow.
He bet with his brother that he would win the race.
This cannot be bet on.

you bet! – *na und ob! aber sicher!*
you can bet your boots on that! – *darauf kannst du Gift nehmen*
you can bet your bottom dollar on that – *darauf kannst du Gift nehmen*

to bet twenty to one – *zwanzig zu eins wetten*
Bet you! – *Wetten!*

Übung

I bet you twenty pounds that I will beat you at golf next time.
Everybody bet on the same horse, which unfortunately came in last.
I'll bet you anything.
Don't bet on it.
Want to bet?

bind bound bound *binden*

She always binds her hair up in a pigtail.
They bound the book with great care.
She was bound to the chair so that she could not move.
The victim was bound hand and foot.

Idioms

to be bound to do something – *zwangsläufig etwas tun müssen*
that was bound to happen – *das musste ja passieren*
I am bound to say – *ich muss sagen*
to be bound up in something – *ganz aufgehen in etwas, ganz in Anspruch genommen sein von etwas*
to bind somebody to something – *jemanden zu etwas verpflichten*
to bind somebody as an apprentice – *jemanden in die Lehre nehmen*

Übung

Can you help me bind up his broken leg?
I could have told you that before – this silly plan was bound to fail.
All the members of our club must be bound to secrecy.

Hinweis

to be snowbound – *eingeschneit, von der Außenwelt abgeschnitten sein*

bite bit bitten *beißen*

Watch out! His dog bites.
The little girl bit into the apple.

I bit off a large piece of his sausage and he got really annoyed.
Have you been bitten by a dog before?

◄ Idioms

to bite off more than one can chew – *sich zu viel zumuten*
to bite back a remark – *sich eine Bemerkung verkneifen*
to bite the dust – *ins Gras beißen*
to bite one's lips – *seinen Ärger hinunterschlucken*
the biter will be bitten – *wer anderen eine Grube gräbt, fällt selbst hinein*
once bitten, twice shy – *ein gebranntes Kind scheut das Feuer*
to bite one's nails – *an seinen Nägeln kauen*
to bite one's tongue – *sich auf die Zunge beißen*
to have been bitten by the travel bug – *vom Reisefieber erwischt worden sein*
to bite the hand that feeds you – *sich ins eigene Fleisch schneiden*
What's biting you? – *Was ist mit dir los?*
She's been bitten. – *Sie ist reingelegt worden.*

◄ Übung

The heavy smoke was biting my eyes.
His face looked terrible – it was badly bitten by the mosquitoes.
We have been here for hours, but the fish simply won't bite.
I don't like people who are biting their nails.
Have you heard about the cat that bit the dog?

bleed bled bled *bluten*

Bleeders bleed easily and do not stop bleeding.
My nose bled very often.
Her wound has bled badly, but it looks better now.

◄ Idioms

my heart bleeds for you – *ich habe großes Mitleid mit dir; (iron.: mir kommen gleich die Tränen)*
to bleed for something – *für etwas schwer bluten müssen*
to bleed someone white – *jemanden völlig ausnehmen, sein ganzes Geld abknöpfen, jemanden auspressen*
to bleed someone for 1000 pounds – *jemandem 1000 Pfund abknöpfen*
to bleed to death – *verbluten*
to bleed somebody dry – *jemanden total ausnehmen*

Übung

Nobody helped them, and so they bled to death.
When he was sick, the doctor came and bled him.
This man bled me dry. I've got no money left.

blend   blended/blent   blended/blent   *(sich)(ver)mischen*

Beachte

"blent" ist eine veraltete Form!

Blend two eggs and some flour together.
We blended our coffee ourselves.
Do you like blended whiskey or do you prefer single malt?
The chef has blended the ingredients for the cake.

Idioms

to blend in (well) with something – *gut passen zu, sich gut verbinden mit etwas, harmonieren miteinander (z.B. Farben)*

Übung

Sea and sky seemed to blend into one another.
They didn't blend this new skyscraper in with its surroundings.
I don't like blending alcohol and milk.

bless   blessed/blest   blessed/blest   *segnen*

Beachte

Die üblichere Form ist, "blessed"!

I asked the priest to bless my baby.
Jesus blessed the children.
My mother has always been blessed with good health.

Idioms

I am blest if I know! – *ich weiß es wirklich nicht!*
to bless oneself – *sich glücklich schätzen*
you may bless your stars that – *sie können von Glück sagen, dass*
Bless my soul! – *Du meine Güte!*
She's done it again, bless her. – *Sie hat es schon wieder getan, na toll.*
I'll be blessed if I'm going to do that! – *Das fällt mir ja im Traum nicht ein!*
Well, I'll be blessed! – *So was!*
to bless somebody with something – *jemanden mit etwas segnen*

God bless you!
Bless you!
God bless America!
Bless you, darling, you're an angel.

blow   blew   blown   *blasen*

Please blow the candle out!
I blew the dust off the shelf.
My uncle is quite an artist – he blows glass.
During the play he blew his nose at least five times.
Then the whistle blew and the game was over.

to blow hot and cold – *das Fähnchen nach dem Winde drehen, unbeständig sein*
to blow off steam – *Dampf ablassen, sich austoben*
to blow one's top – *vor Wut explodieren, in die Luft gehen*
to blow up – *die Beherrschung verlieren*
to blow someone up – *jemanden herunterputzen*
to blow something up into – *etwas aufbauschen zu*
There she blows! – *Wal in Sicht!*
to blow one's own trumpet – *sein eigenes Lob singen*
to be blown to pieces – *in die Luft gesprengt werden; zerfetzt werden*
Blow this rain! – *Dieser verdammte Regen!*
Well, I'll be blowed! – *Menschenskind!*
I'll be blowed if I'll do it! – *Ich denke nicht im Traum daran, das zu tun.*
to blow one's chances of doing something – *es sich verscherzen, etwas zu tun*
I think I've blown it! – *Ich glaube, ich habs versaut!*
to blow away – *wegwehen, wegblasen*
to blow down – *umgeweht werden, umfallen*
to blow somebody's head off – *jemandem eine Kugel durch den Kopf jagen*
to blow out – *ausgehen, ausblasen*

She had a bad cold and blew her nose all the time.
This is a nice photograph of you. We should get it blown up.
Thank God, the storm has finally blown over.
The wind was blowing hard.
Suddenly the door blew open.

The wind blew the ship off course.
He's blown a fuse.
The car blew a tyre. That's why we had to stop.

> to blow the whistle on someone (bes. AE) – *jemanden „verpfeifen"*

break   broke   broken   *brechen*

Be careful, this wine glass breaks easily.
Last week he went skiing and broke his leg.
I am very disappointed because she has broken her word.

to break the ice – *das Eis brechen*
to break new ground – *etwas machen, was noch niemand gemacht hat; Neuland betreten*
to break the news to someone – *jemandem eine Neuigkeit schonend mitteilen*
to break someone of a habit – *jemandem etwas abgewöhnen*
to break up a relationship – *eine Beziehung beenden*
to break something from something – *etwas von etwas abbrechen*
to break bail – *die Haftverschonung brechen*
to break a holiday short – *einen Urlaub abbrechen*
to break a habit – *sich etwas abgewöhnen*
to break somebody (financially) – *jemanden ruinieren; jemanden in den Bankrott treiben*
to break the bank – *die Bank sprengen*
to break step – *aus dem Schritt kommen*
to break for lunch – *Mittagspause machen*
to break from jail – *aus dem Gefängnis ausbrechen*
to break even – *seine Unkosten decken*
to break away from the everyday routine – *aus dem Alltagstrott ausbrechen*
to break down – *scheitern; zusammenbrechen; aufgliedern*
to break forth – *losbrechen; hervorbrechen*
to break off – *abbrechen; aufhören*
to break through somebody's reserve – *jemanden aus der Reserve locken*
to break out in a rash – *einen Ausschlag bekommen*
Break it up! – *Auseinander!*

He broke her heart when he left her. ◀ **Übung**
I am sure he will break the world record next year.
At the French border our old car broke down.
When the war broke out, we left the country.
When she left him, his spirit broke.
His voice is beginning to break.
When did the party break up last night?

breed   bred   bred   *züchten; hervorrufen*

My uncle breeds horses in his leisure time.
The unjust distribution of wealth bred hatred.
Did you know that they have bred a new variety of flower?
Dirt breeds disease.

to breed like rabbits – *sich wie Kaninchen vermehren*   ◀ **Idioms**
to breed bad (ill) blood between – *böses Blut schaffen zwischen*

Most birds breed in the spring.   ◀ **Übung**
I only go out with well-bred young men.
Violence breeds only more violence.

> bred in the bone – *angeboren (z.B. Eigenschaft)*   ◀ **Hinweis**

bring   brought   brought   *bringen*

Please take the empty bottle away and bring me a full one.
They always brought their seven children with them.
I have brought some friends along for dinner.
Two days ago she brought a present to her mother.
He can't bring himself to speak to her.
The trial will be brought next month.

to bring someone to his senses – *jemanden zur Vernunft bringen*   ◀ **Idioms**
to bring someone down to earth – *jemanden auf den Boden der Tatsachen zurückholen*
to bring about a change – *eine Veränderung bewirken, mit sich bringen*
to bring something up – *etwas zur Sprache bringen*
to bring up children – *Kinder großziehen*

to bring the house down – *Zuschauer zu begeistertem Applaus hinreißen*
to bring something to light – *etwas aufdecken, ans Tageslicht bringen*
to bring down the government – *die Regierung stürzen*
to bring someone down – *jemanden zur Strecke bringen*
to bring something into ply – *etwas ins Spiel bringen*
to bring something into the open – *etwas ans Tageslicht bringen*
to bring tears to somebody's eyes – *jemandem die Tränen in die Augen treiben*
to bring something to a close – *etwas zu Ende bringen*
to bring something to an end – *etwas zu Ende bringen*
to bring somebody low – *jemanden auf Null bringen*
to bring something to somebody's knowledge – *jemandem etwas zur Kenntnis bringen*
to bring something to somebody's attention – *jemanden auf etwas aufmerksam machen*
to bring to perfection – *vervollkommnen*
to bring about – *wenden (Schiff)*
to bring somebody back to life – *jemanden wieder lebendig machen*
to bring a government back to power – *eine Regierung wieder an die Macht bringen*
to bring somebody's wrath down upon one – *sich jemandes Zorn zuziehen*
to bring forth – *hervorbringen; zur Welt bringen*
Why bring that in? – *Was hat das damit zu tun?*
to bring into view – *sichtbar werden lassen*
to bring off a coup – *ein Ding drehen*
to bring something upon oneself – *sich etwas selbst aufladen*
to bring the worst in somebody – *das Schlimmste in jemandem zum Vorschein bringen*
to bring somebody out in spots – *bei jemandem Pickel verursachen*
to bring somebody to himself/herself – *jemanden wieder zu sich bringen*
to bring somebody up to do something – *jemanden dazu erziehen, etwas zu tun*
to bring something up – *etwas zur Sprache bringen*
to bring somebody up against something – *jemanden mit etwas konfrontieren*
to bring to pass – *zustande bringen*

We must bring the matter to a close soon.
Don't bring her into it.
Your remark brought tears to her eyes.

build   built   built   *bauen*

The Eskimos built their igloos out of icy blocks of snow.
He built up his business within two years.
Near our village a new railway will be built.
So far he has built five houses in his life.

to build one's hopes on – *seine Hoffnungen setzen auf*
to build castles in the air – *Luftschlösser bauen*
to build up one's health – *seine Gesundheit festigen*
to build something onto something – *etwas an etwas anbauen*
to build up a reputation – *sich einen Namen machen*
to build up somebody's hopes – *jemandem Hoffnungen machen*
built on sand – *auf Sand gebaut*

The whole building was built of wood.
This camera has a built-in-flash.
He is a well-built man.
He never does what he says, so do not build on him.
The house is being built.
The parts build up into a complete cupboard.
Lots of dumplings build you up.

burn burnt/burned
burnt/burned   *brennen, verbrennen*

Dry wood burns better than wet wood.
She burnt all her English books.
The child has burnt her fingers.
I'm sure he'll burn in hell.

to be burning to do something – *darauf brennen etwas zu tun*
to burn one's boats – *alle Brücken hinter sich abbrechen*
to burn the midnight oil – *bis spät in die Nacht aufbleiben und arbeiten (lernen)*

to burn the candle at both ends – *sich übernehmen, sich Tag und Nacht keine Ruhe gönnen*
to burn to the ground – *völlig abbrennen (Haus)*
to be burnt at the stake – *auf dem Scheiterhaufen verbrannt werden*
to be burnt to death – *verbrannt werden; verbrennen*
to be burnt alive – *bei lebendigem Leibe verbrannt werden*
to burn one's fingers – *sich die Finger verbrennen*
He's got money to burn. – *Er hat Geld wie Heu.*
to burn up the road – *die Straße entlangbrausen*
to be burned up with envy – *sich vor Neid verzehren*

Übung ▶

Burning with anger, he left his office.
You will burn yourself out if you work too hard.
I let the candle burn out.
Her skin burns easily.
The acid burned into the surface.
Her face was burning with shame when she saw her sister.

Beachte ▶

to burn someone up (AE) – *jemanden ausschimpfen*
to get burned up (AE) – *wütend werden*

burst   burst   burst   *bersten, platzen*

She is so fat that she bursts out of her dresses.
Suddenly the balloon burst.
I would have burst if I had eaten another piece of the cake.

Idioms ▶

to burst in on someone – *bei jemandem hereinplatzen; sich in eine Unterhaltung einmischen*
to burst into flames – *in Flammen aufgehen*
to burst into laughter/tears – *in Gelächter/Tränen ausbrechen*
to burst into leaf – *ins Laub schießen (Bäume)*
to burst out of prison – *ausbrechen*
to burst with laughter – *sich vor Lachen schütteln*
to burst with pride – *voller Stolz sein*
to burst with energy – *vor Energie strotzen*
to burst open – *aufspringen; aufbrechen; aufplatzen*
to be full to bursting – *zum Platzen voll sein*
to be bursting with health – *vor Gesundheit strotzen*
to burst through the enemy lines – *die feindlichen Linien durchbrechen*

to burst into view – *plötzlich in Sicht kommen*
to burst into song – *lossingen*
to burst into bloom – *plötzlich aufblühen*
to burst in on somebody – *bei jemandem hereinplatzen*
to burst in fury – *plötzlich vom Leder ziehen*
to burst crying – *in Tränen ausbrechen*

Please tell me about it – I am bursting with curiosity.
Unexpectedly my mother burst into the room.
"That's not true!", she burst out.
She was bursting to tell us.
The river has burst its banks.

buy   bought   bought   *kaufen*

Money cannot buy happiness.
Our second-hand shop buys and sells books.
My parents bought me a racing car.
I have finally bought a new pair of shoes.

to buy time – *Zeit gewinnen*
to buy something for a song – *etwas ganz billig erstehen*
I don't buy that! – *Das kaufe ich dir nicht ab, glaube ich dir nicht!*
He bought it! – *Den hat's erwischt!*
to buy out – *loskaufen; freikaufen*
to buy over – *für sich gewinnen*

I bought the house from a friend of mine.
The company has bought up all publishers in the city.
Did you manage to buy him over?

cast   cast   cast   *werfen*

She is very shy and always casts her eyes down.
The building cast a shadow.
We have cast the nets but have not caught any fish yet.
She was well cast. Lady Macbeth was the perfect role for her.

to cast about for something – *sich umsehen nach, suchen nach etwas*

19

to cast a burden on someone – *jemandem eine Last aufbürden*
to cast the blame on someone – *jemandem die Schuld zuschieben (vgl. to lay/put the blame on someone)*
to cast dust in someone's eyes – *jemandem Sand in die Augen streuen*
the die is cast – *die Würfel sind gefallen*
to cast a spell on someone – *jemanden verzaubern*
to be cast down – *niedergeschlagen sein*
to cast light on something – *Licht werfen auf, zur Klärung beitragen (vgl. to shed light on something)*
to cast pearls before swine – *Perlen vor die Säue werfen*
to cast an eye over something – *sich etwas kurz anschauen, Blick werfen auf*
to cast a vote – *seine Stimme abgeben*
to cast lots – *(aus)losen*
to cast in one's lot with somebody – *sich auf jemandes Seite stellen*
to cast its skin – *sich häuten*
to cast a shoe – *ein Hufeisen verlieren*
to cast its feathers – *sich mausern*
to cast its leaves – *die Blätter abwerfen*
to cast its young – *(Junge) werfen*
to cast oneself as – *sich darstellen als*
to cast aside – *ausrangieren; ablegen*
to be cast away – *gestrandet sein*
to cast back in one's mind – *im Geiste zurückdenken*
to cast off – *fallen lassen; losmachen*
to cast something up at somebody – *jemandem etwas vorhalten*

She has changed very much: She has cast aside all her inhibitions.
We will cast anchor near the store.
The horse cast a show yesterday.
To impress his future mother-in-law he cast himself as a bank director.

catch   caught   caught　　　　　　*fangen*

Come one, try to catch me!
My Dad caught a lot of fish on Saturday.
The police have caught the thieves.

to catch someone red-handed – *jemanden auf frischer Tat ertappen* ◀ Idioms
to catch someone's eye – *jemandes Aufmerksamkeit auf sich lenken*
to catch one's breath – *wieder zu Atem kommen; den Atem anhalten*
to catch sight of someone – *jemanden kurz erblicken*
to catch up with someone – *jemanden einholen*
to catch on – *Mode werden, Anklang finden*
to catch a glimpse of somebody – *jemanden zu sehen kriegen*
to catch somebody's attention – *jemanden auf sich aufmerksam machen*
to be caught between two alternatives – *zwischen zwei Möglichkeiten hin und her gerissen sein*
to catch somebody at something – *jemanden bei etwas erwischen*
to catch somebody by surprise – *jemanden überraschen*
to be caught unprepared – *nicht darauf vorbereitet sein*
to catch somebody at a bad time – *jemandem ungelegen kommen*
aha, caught you – *hab ich dich doch erwischt*
caught in the act – *auf frischer Tat ertappt*
to catch somebody off balance – *jemanden überrumpeln*
to catch an illness – *sich eine Krankheit holen*
You'll catch your death! – *Du holst dir den Tod!*
You'll catch it! – *Du kannst aber was erleben!*
He caught it all right! – *Der hat aber was zu hören bekommen!*
I caught you out there! – *Du bist durchschaut!*
to catch up on one's sleep – *Schlaf nachholen*
to catch up with one's work – *Arbeit nachholen*
to catch up the skirts – *die Röcke schürzen*
to get caught up in something – *sich in etwas verheddern; in etwas verwickelt werden*

I feel very bad because I have caught a terrible cold. ◀ Übung
Hurry up, we must catch the train in five minutes!
Sorry, but I do not quite catch what you have said.
He held the picture up to catch the light.
You won't catch me falling for that trick again.
A nail caught her bag.
Why is he screaming? He caught his finger in the door.
The burglar was caught in the act.

21

choose   chose   chosen   *wählen*

You can choose a restaurant. I do not mind where we go.
They could choose between a trip to Singapore and a new television set.
There are ten different models to choose from.
My mother chose a green dress for me.
I hope you have chosen your friends carefully.

Idioms ▶

Do as you chose! – *Tu, was dir beliebt/gefällt!*
There is not much to choose between them. – *Es ist kaum ein Unterschied zwischen ihnen.*
We cannot choose but do it – *Es bleibt uns keine andere Wahl, als es zu tun*
not choose to do something – *nicht geruhen, etwas zu tun*
to choose a team – *eine Mannschaft zusammenstellen*
well-chosen words – *wohlgesetzte Worte*

Übung ▶

I chose to stay home since the weather was so bad.
The politician chose his words carefully when he criticised the government.
He was chosen spokesman of the committee.

Hinweis ▶

the chosen people – *das auserwählte Volk (Bibel)*

cling   clung   clung   *sich klammern an*

I still cling to belief that he will not die.
I clung to his arm when he walked through the snowstorm.
The little girl clung to her mother's skirt.
We had always clung to the hope that he would be saved.

Idioms ▶

to cling together – *zusammenhalten (Menschen); zusammenkleben (Dinge)*
Cling on tight! – *Halt dich gut fest!*

Übung ▶

The smell of cigarette smoke clung to his clothes.
When she translates, she clings to the text too much.
It had been raining and my wet shirt clung to my body.
The two women cling together since their early childhood.

come came come *kommen*

My brother comes to see me every weekend.
We came here by bus.
I am getting worried because he still has not come.
Shall I come with you to the appointment?
Finally her dreams came true.

◄ Idioms

to come about – *geschehen, passieren, zustande kommen*
to come round – *bei jemandem kurz „vorbeischauen", jemanden besuchen*
to come in handy – *nützlich sein, wie gerufen kommen*
to come into fashion – *in Mode kommen*
to come off – *abgehen, sich lösen (z.B. Knopf)*
to come to grips with something – *sich ernsthaft auseinandersetzen mit etwas*
to come to the conclusion that – *zu dem Schluss kommen, dass*
to come to the fore as – *sich hervortun als (in positivem Sinne)*
to come to one's senses – *zur Besinnung kommen, wieder zur Vernunft kommen*
to come to the point – *zur Sache kommen*
to come to a head – *sich zuspitzen (Lage, Situation)*
to come to terms with someone – *sich einigen mit jemandem*
to come to terms with something – *etwas bewältigen, mit etwas fertig werden*
to come under fire – *unter Beschuss geraten, mit Worten angegriffen werden*
to come up with something – *daherkommen mit, präsentieren (z.B. Idee, Plan, Lösung)*
come to think of it ... – *wenn ich es mir so recht überlege ...*
come what may – *was auch immer geschieht; komme, was wolle*
in the years to come – *in den kommenden Jahren*
Come off it! – *Hör schon auf damit! Gib nicht so an! Tu nicht so!*
Come and get it! – *Essen fassen!*
Coming! – *Ich komm ja schon!*
Come now! – *Na, na!*
it came to me that ..., – *mir fiel ein, dass ...*
come what may – *ganz gleich, was geschieht*
How come? – *Wieso?*

now I come to think of it – *wenn ich es mir recht überlege*
this is how it came about ... – *das ist so gekommen ...*
to come across with – *rausrücken mit*
Come along with me. – *Kommen Sie bitte mit.*
to be coming along – *sich machen; vorangehen*
to come apart – *kaputtgehen; auseinanderfallen*
It's all coming back. – *Jetzt erinnere ich mich wieder.*
when you come down to it – *letzten Endes*
to come with help – *Hilfe anbieten*
to come in fourth – *Vierter werden*
That will come in handy. – *Das kann man noch gut gebrauchen.*
Nothing came of it. – *Es ist nichts daraus geworden.*
Come off it! – *Nun mach mal halblang!*
Winter is coming on. – *Es wird Winter.*
to come out fighting – *sich kämpferisch geben*
to come out in favour of something – *sich für etwas aussprechen*
to come round to doing something – *dazu kommen, etwas zu tun*
It comes to the same thing. – *Das läuft auf dasselbe hinaus.*

Übung ▶

We came to know each other on the plane to London.
One day my dreams will come true.
When I read the manuscript, I came across a lot of typing mistakes.
Why don't you come along to the concert?
How is your English coming along?
Come and see me soon.
He has come a long way.
Be careful. The handle has come loose.
Everything came all right in the end.
Their case came before the courts.
His brother has come down in the world a bit.
The water came up to her knees.

cost   cost   cost   *kosten*

It doesn't cost much to eat at a fast food restaurant.
The new carpet in the living-room cost me 500 pounds.
Her carelessness almost cost her her life.
It has cost me a lot of time to prepare this delicious dinner.

to cost someone dearly – *jemanden teuer zu stehen kommen*
to cost the earth – *ein Heidengeld kosten*
to cost an arm and a leg – *einen zu hohen Preis haben*
cost what it may – *koste es, was es wolle*
at all costs – *um jeden Preis*
cost a packet (AE) – *extrem teuer*

◀ Idioms

These shoes cost a fortune! I do not think I can afford to buy them.
His fancy for fast cars has cost him his life.
How much will it cost to have it repaired?

◀ Übung

> In der Bedeutung „*Kosten kalkulieren, veranschlagen*" wird die Form "costed" verwendet:
> z.B.: "The working hours were costed at 200 pounds."

◀ Beachte

creep   crept   crept   *kriechen; schleichen*

I tried to creep into my room before my mother saw me.
I crept under the table to pick up my pencil.
The beetle has crept over the stone.

to make someone's flesh creep – *jemandem eine Gänsehaut machen, verursachen (vgl.* to give someone the creeps)
to creep into someone's favour – *sich bei jemandem einschmeicheln*
to creep over someone – *einen beschleichen (z.B. Angst)*
to creep up – *langsam steigen (z.B. Auflage einer Zeitung, Preise etc.)*
to creep up on someone – *sich an jemanden heranschleichen*
to creep back – *wieder angekrochen kommen*
to creep over – *beschleichen; überkommen*

◀ Idioms

How did this mistake creep into your work?
Two weeks after their divorce he crept back.
The tiger crept up on his quarry.

◀ Übung

> creeper – *Kletterpflanze, Kriechtier;* creep – *Kriecher, Schleimer;* creepy – *gruselig, unheimlich;* creeping – *schleichend*

◀ Hinweis

cut cut cut *schneiden*

We will cut the birthday-cake into twelve pieces.
He cut his finger when he tried to open the tin.
I had my hair cut on Friday.
The grass had not been cut for many months.

Idioms ▶

to cut something – *etwas verringern, herabsetzen, einschränken (z.B. Produktion, Ausgaben)*
to cut corners – *die Kurven schneiden (bes. Auto)*
to cut one's coat according to one's cloth – *sich nach der Decke strecken*
to cut down a tree – *einen Baum fällen*
to cut a long story short – *um es kurz zu machen, kurz und gut*
to cut both ways – *ein zweischneidiges Schwert sein, seine Vor- und Nachteile haben*
to cut in fine – *in Zeitnot, Geldnot u.Ä. kommen*
to cut someone dead – *jemanden „schneiden", links liegen lassen, nicht beachten, völlig ignorieren*
to cut someone to the heart – *jemanden sehr betrügen, ins Herz schneiden*
to cut no ice with someone – *bei jemandem keinen Eindruck machen*
to cut someone down to size – *jemanden zurechtweisen, den Kopf zurechtsetzen*
to cut someone off without a penny – *jemanden enterben*
to cut off someone's escape – *jemandem den Rückzug abschneiden*
to cut off one's nose to spite one's face – *sich ins eigene Fleisch schneiden*
to be cut for something – *für etwas wie geschaffen sein*
to cut the ground from under someone's feet – *jemandem den Boden unter den Füßen wegziehen*
Cut it out! – *Hör auf damit! Lass den Quatsch!*
to get one's hair cut – *sich die Haare schneiden lassen*
to cut a fine figure – *eine gute Figur abgeben*
to cut the cards – *abheben*
to cut and run – *die Beine in die Hand nehmen*

It was very impolite of him to cut into the conversation.
I have just cut out the most interesting articles out of the magazine.
Stone does not cut as easily as paper.

to cut up (AE) – *angeben, Quatsch machen* ◀ Beachte

deal dealt dealt *(be)handeln*

This book deals with the history of America.
My aunt's shop dealt in sports wear.
So far we have dealt in hardware, but now we deal in software, too.

to deal cards – *Karten geben, austeilen* ◀ Idioms
to deal with someone – *mit jemandem verkehren, zu tun haben*
to deal with something – *sich mit etwas befassen; mit etwas fertig werden, zu Rande kommen, erledigen*
to deal with a case – *einen Fall verhandeln*
to deal out criticism – *Kritik üben*
to deal fairly with someone – *jdn anständig behandeln*
to deal a blow at someone – *jdm einen Schlag versetzen*

Let's deal this topic first. ◀ Übung
We deal only in facts.
They dealt out punishment to the men.

a great deal of something – *eine Menge, viel* ◀ Hinweis
it is a big deal – *eine „große Sache" sein*

dig dug dug *graben*

We will dig a hole to see whether there is a treasure hidden in the ground.
The dog dug a deep hole in the garden.
We have not dug deep enough yet.

to dig one's own garden – *sich sein eigenes Grab schaufeln* ◀ Idioms
to dig something up – *etwas herauskramen, aufstöbern, finden*
to dig somebody in the ribs – *jemanden in die Rippen stoßen*
to dig for minerals – *Erz schürfen*
to dig deep into one's pockets – *tief in die Taschen greifen*
Dig in! – *Hau rein! (Aufforderung zum Essen)*

Übung

Stop digging me in the ribs!
They dug their way out of prison.
He had to dig deep to remember her name.

dive   dived/dove   dived   *(ein)tauchen*

Beachte

> Nur im AE ist die Form "dove" üblich, sonst ist
> das Verb regelmäßig.

It is too dangerous to dive here because there are many sharks.
I dived/dove into the pool from the springboard.
The submarine has dived again.

Idioms

to dive into the crowd – *in der Menge untertauchen*
to dive for the ball – *nach dem Ball hechten*
to dive under the table – *blitzschnell unter dem Tisch verschwinden*
to dive for cover – *schnell in Deckung gehen*
Dive in! – *Hau rein! (Aufforderung zum Essen; vgl.* dig in!)

Übung

I dived/dove into my pocket and pulled out the key.
She dived into the crowd.
These boys dive for pearls.

do   did   done   *tun, machen*

If he does that again, I will punish him.
It is sometimes difficult to do the right thing at the right time.
Did you do your homework?
I have not done anything exiting during the past few days.

Idioms

to do away with something – *etwas beseitigen; abschaffen*
to do away with someone – *jemanden töten*
to do business with someone – *mit jemandem Geschäfte machen*
to do one's bit – *seinen Betrag leisten, seine Pflicht tun*
I could do with something – *ich könnte etwas gut gebrauchen, etwas würde mir gut tun*
to do someone a favour – *jemandem einen Gefallen tun*
to do someone harm – *jemandem schaden, etwas antun*

to do someone in – *jemanden umbringen*
to be done for – *erledigt sein, am Ende sein*
to do without something – *auf etwas verzichten*
to do badly (well) – *Erfolg haben, gut abschneiden (z.B. Prüfung)*
to do justice to someone/something – *jemandem/einer Sache Gerechtigkeit widerfahren lassen, gerecht werden*
to do the dishes – *Geschirr spülen*
to do up the house – *das Haus renovieren, reparieren*
to do oneself up – *sich herrichten, zurechtmachen*
to do up one's face – *sich schminken*
Nothing doing! – *Da ist nichts zu machen, kommt nicht in Frage!*
That will do! – *Das genügt, das reicht!*

That's easier said than done.
I did my best. Yet I was not successful.
What have you done to your hair? It looks so different today.
Drink this, it will do you good.

◄ **Übung**

> Das Verb "do" wird natürlich auch als Hilfsverb gebraucht!

◄ **Beachte**

draw   drew   drawn   *ziehen; zeichnen*

My brother is quite an artist; he draws very beautiful pictures.
Last week the dentist drew three of my teeth.
Look, we have drawn a map of Britain.

to draw alongside – *nahe heranfahren an etwas*
to draw apart – *sich auseinander leben (Personen)*
to draw someone's attention to something – *jemandes Aufmerksamkeit auf etwas lenken*
to draw something to a close – *etwas zu Ende bringen, abschließen*
to draw on something – *in Anspruch nehmen, zurückgreifen auf, angreifen (z.B. Ersparnisse)*
to draw a cheque on one's bank account – *einen Scheck einlösen*
to draw the line at something – *die Grenze ziehen bei, bei etwas nicht mehr mitmachen*

◄ **Idioms**

to draw near – *näher kommen (zeitlich und örtlich)*
to draw up (car) – *vorfahren (das Auto)*
with drawn sword – *mit gezogenem Schwert*
to draw a long breath – *einmal tief Luft holen*
to draw strength from something – *Kraft aus etwas schöpfen*
to draw fire – *das Feuer auf sich lenken*
to feel drawn towards somebody – *sich zu jemandem hingezogen fühlen*
to draw a match – *unentschieden spielen*
to draw round the table – *sich um den Tisch versammeln*

When the light is on my room, I always draw the curtains.
You cannot draw a comparison between my life in Africa and life in Europe.
What conclusions have you drawn from this?
You have to draw a distinction between my personal opinion and what I say in public.

dream dreamt/dreamed dreamt/dreamed *träumen*

I dream every night.
We dream of going to Alaska for our next holiday.
She closed her eyes and dreamt of better times.
I have dreamt about you.
I never dreamt that he would do such a thing.

to dream away the hours/the time – *Zeit verträumen, vertun*
to dream something up – *sich etwas zusammenfantasieren, sich etwas ausdenken*

In my youth I dreamt many dreams.
He saw that I could not manage on my own, but he did not dream of helping me.
I never said such a thing! You must have dreamt that!
Who would have dreamt it would be so complicated.

drink drank drunk   *trinken*

He drinks a lot. He is almost an alcoholic.
Our dog drank out of a puddle.

I was so thirsty that I could have drunk a whole bottle of water.
She has already drunk your lemonade.

◄ Idioms

to drink something away – *etwas versaufen (Geld); etwas in Alkohol ertränken (Sorgen)*
to drink someone under the table – *jemanden unter den Tisch trinken*
to drink in someone's words – *jemandes Wort gierig aufsaugen*
to drink in the air – *Luft einatmen, einsaugen*
to drink in the view – *den Augenblick genießen*
to go out drinking – *einen trinken gehen*
drinking and driving – *Alkohol am Steuer*
to drink to something – *auf etwas trinken*
to drink down – *hinuntertrinken; hinunterschlucken*

◄ Übung

Drink your wine up, we want to go home.
We drank to his health three times.
I did not marry him because he drank.
I'll drink to that.

drive   drove   driven   *fahren; treiben*

My father never let me drive, even though I had a driving licence.
We drove home very late last night.
I have driven Japanese cars all my life.
The heavy storm has driven the clouds away.
The ship was driven by steam-power.

◄ Idioms

to drive someone nuts – *jemanden wahnsinnig, verrückt machen*
to drive someone crazy/mad – *jemanden verrückt machen, auf die Palme bringen*
to drive someone round the bend – *jemanden verrückt machen*
to drive something home to someone – *jemandem etwas klarmachen*
to be driving at something – *auf etwas hinauswollen, auf etwas anspielen*
to drive someone into a corner – *jemanden in die Enge treiben*

to drive somebody out of the country – *jemanden aus dem Land (ver)treiben*
to drive a nail into something – *einen Nagel in etwas treiben*
to drive somebody very hard – *jemanden sehr hart rannehmen*
to drive on the right – *rechts fahren*

Übung

Finally we managed to drive the nail into the wall.
When the traffic-lights turned green, they drove on.
I was driven to it.

eat ate eaten *essen*

Don't eat too much before you go swimming!
At home we ate roast chicken every Sunday.
Sorry, there is nothing left of the pie; we have just eaten the last piece of it.

Idioms

to eat like a sparrow/bird – *wie ein Spatz essen, sehr wenig essen*
to eat like a horse – *wie ein Scheunendrescher essen*
to eat one's hat – *einen Besen fressen*
to eat one's words – *Gesagtes zurücknehmen, widerrufen*
to eat in – *zuhause essen*
to eat out – *essen gehen*
to eat one's way through – *sich durch(fr)essen*
to eat somebody out of house and home – *jemandem die Haare vom Kopf fressen*
to eat one's heart out – *Trübsal blasen*
What's eating him? – *Was für eine Laus ist ihm über die Leber gelaufen? Was hat er denn?*

Übung

When she heard about his success, she was eaten up with jealousy.
I get on with him very well because he eats out of my hand.
He won't eat you!

fall fell fallen *fallen*

The temperature will fall eight degrees tonight.
She fell off the horse and broke her leg.
I have fallen down and hurt my head.

to fall in love with someone – *sich in jemanden verlieben*
to fall out of love with someone – *nicht mehr in jemanden verliebt sein, jemanden nicht mehr lieben*
to fall for someone – *sich in jemanden verlieben*
to fall through – *nichts werden, ins Wasser fallen*
to fall flat – *schief gehen, danebengehen*
to fall back on something – *auf etwas zurückgreifen, einen Rückhalt haben an etwas*
to fall behind someone – *hinter jemandem zurückbleiben, ins Hintertreffen geraten*
to fall over oneself to do something – *sich überschlagen, etwas zu tun; etwas mit besonderem Eifer tun*
to fall to one's death – *tödlich abstürzen*
to fall into a trap – *in die Falle gehen*
her eyes fell – *sie schlug die Augen nieder*
his face fell – *er machte ein langes Gesicht*
to fall in somebody's estimation – *in jemandes Achtung sinken*
to fall into four sections – *sich in vier Teile gliedern*
to fall asleep – *einschlafen*
to fall pregnant – *schwanger werden*
to fall into decay – *verfallen*
to fall into temptation – *in Versuchung geraten*
to fall into conversation with somebody – *mit jemandem ins Gespräch kommen*
to fall among thieves – *unter die Räuber geraten*
to fall in beside somebody – *sich jemandem anschließen*
when Adam fell – *nach Adams Sündenfall*

The lesson was so boring that she soon fell asleep.
Be careful! The book will fall apart if you open it.
I really fell into the role of this character.

feed fed fed   *füttern*

Please do not feed the swans here! They will grow too fat.
At the zoo we were allowed to feed some of the animals.
I have fed the birds with sunflower seeds.
When my father was ill, I fed him the meals.
Raw meat was fed to the tigers.

to feed the cows – *die Kühe weiden lassen*
to feed at the breast – *ein Kind stillen*

to feed on something – *etwas essen, sich ernähren von*
to feed one's eyes on something – *seine Augen weiden an etwas*
to feed someone up – *jemanden aufpäppeln*
to be fed up with something/someone – *genug von etwas/jemandem haben*
to bite the hand that feeds you – *sich den eigenen Ast absägen*
to feed oneself – *sich selbst verpflegen*
to feed information to somebody – *jemanden mit Informationen versorgen*
to feed somebody with the right lines – *jemandem das richtige Stichwort geben*
to feed in – *einführen; eingeben*
to feed somebody up – *jemanden aufpäppeln*

She earned so little money that she could not even feed her family.
I fed the data into the computer.
The ducks in the park fed out of my hand.
The prisoners were fed to the lions.

feel felt felt *(sich)(an)fühlen*

I have made such a stupid mistake – I feel like an idiot.
She washed her jumper with a new detergent – it felt wonderfully soft afterwards.
I have never felt so bad in all my life.
After the long walk we all felt extremely tired.

to feel like doing something – *Lust haben, etwas zu tun*
to feel up to something – *sich zu etwas aufraffen können, in der Stimmung sein zu etwas; einer Sache gewachsen sein*
to feel out of place – *sich fehl am Platze fühlen*
to feel one's way – *sich vorwärts tasten; vorsichtig vorgehen*
to feel angry – *wütend, ärgerlich sein*
to feel cold – *frieren*
to feel blue – *traurig sein*
to feel about something – *eine Meinung haben über etwas*
to feel sorry for someone – *jemand tut einem Leid*
to feel rough – *sich rau anfühlen*

to feel like – *Lust haben*
to get a feel for something – *ein Gefühl für etwas bekommen*
to feel about – *umhertasten; herumsuchen*
to feel up to – *sich gewachsen fühlen*
I felt that! – *Das hat wehgetan!*
it was felt that ... – *man war der Meinung, dass ...*

I have always felt that there is something wrong with him.
Feel free to say what to think!
He didn't feel up to this new task.

fight   fought   fought   *(be)kämpfen*

We should all try to fight poverty in the Third World.
Japan fought against the USA in World War II.
India had fought for its freedom for many years before it became independent of the British.

to fight it out – *etwas untereinander ausfechten*
to fight back one's tears – *Tränen unterdrücken*
to fight a losing battle – *eine verlorene Schlacht schlagen*
to fight tooth and nail to do something – *mit aller Kraft um etwas kämpfen*
to fight one's way (through) – *sich seinen Weg bahnen, sich durchschlagen*
to fight against disease – *Krankheiten bekämpfen*
to fight for what one believes in – *für seine Überzeugungen eintreten*
to fight for one's life – *um sein Leben kämpfen*
to fight for breath – *nach Atem ringen*
to fight shy of something – *einer Sache aus dem Weg gehen*
to fight a duel – *ein Duell austragen*
to fight an action – *einen Prozess durchfechten*
to fight an election – *kandidieren*
to fight off sleep – *gegen den Schlaf ankämpfen*

Why didn't he fight back when the guy attacked him?
My parents often fought over silly matters.
He was fighting for his life.

find found found *finden*

I find her new dress very attractive. What about you?
In the nineteenth century the gold-diggers found a lot of gold in Alaska.
I have just found out that I have failed my exam.
I have been looking for my pen all over the place but I have not found it yet.

Idioms

to find someone out – *jemanden ertappen*
to find one's feet – *sich eingewöhnen, zurechtkommen*
to find one's way – *seinen Weg finden*
to find somebody away – *jemanden nicht zu Hause antreffen*
to find somebody guilty – *jemanden für schuldig befinden*
to find somebody not guilty – *jemanden freisprechen*
to find and replace – *finden und ersetzen (Text)*
to find for the accused – *den Angeklagten freisprechen*
to find out about something – *etwas entdecken*
you must take us as you find us – *du musst uns nehmen, wie wir sind*

Übung

I have been in New York for half a year now and I can find my way round.
Eventually we found a solution to the problem.
It annoys me that you never find the time to ring me up.

Beachte

> Man darf dieses Verb nicht verwechseln mit:
> "found/founded/founded" – *gründen*.

flee fled fled *fliehen*

He is such a coward! He flees every danger immediately.
As soon as we attacked them, the enemies fled.
He was hunted by the police and fled the country.
Please help me! I have just fled from a murderer.

Idioms

to flee from temptation – *der Versuchung entfliehen*

Übung

As they wanted to beat him, the little boy fled to me.
He fled when he saw the detective.
The animal fled from the hunter.

fling   flung   flung   *werfen, schleudern*

Don't fling yourself into the chair like that!
I flung myself into his arms and kissed him.
I have flung the stone at the cat but I have missed her.

to fling oneself at someone – *sich auf jemanden stürzen; sich jemandem an den Hals werfen*
to fling something in someone's teeth – *jemandem etwas ins Gesicht schleudern (Bemerkung)*
to fling to the winds – *(einen guten Rat) in den Wind schlagen*
to fling the window open – *das Fenster aufstoßen*
to fling a coat round one's shoulder – *sich einen Mantel über die Schulter werfen*
to fling oneself into a task – *sich in eine Aufgabe stürzen*
to fling oneself off a bridge – *sich von einer Brücke stürzen*
to fling oneself to the ground – *sich auf den Boden werfen*
to fling away money – *Geld vergeuden*
to fling one's arms up in horror – *entsetzt die Hände über dem Kopf zusammenschlagen*
to fling something up at somebody – *jemandem etwas unter die Nase reiben*

◄ Idioms

She ran towards him and flung her arms around his neck.
The door was flung open and in came the headmaster.
My mother flung her arms up in horror. I think she didn't like my new trousers.

◄ Übung

fly   flew   flown   *fliegen*

Do you know how to fly a plane?
I will never forget the day when we flew over the Grand Canyon.
The parcels were flown from Munich to London.

to fly high – *ehrgeizig sein, hoch gesteckte Ziele haben, hoch hinauswollen*
to fly at someone – *auf jemanden losgehen*
to fly off the handle – *aus der Haut fahren*
to let fly at someone – *grob werden gegen jemanden*
I must fly – *ich muss schleunigst weg*
Time flies! – *Wie die Zeit vergeht!*

to fly to somebody's side – *an jemandes Seite eilen*
to fly into a rage – *einen Wutanfall bekommen*
to go flying – *hinfallen; runterfallen*
to fly in the face of authority – *sich über jede Autorität hinwegsetzen*
to fly in the face of reason – *jeder Vernunft entbehren*
to fly off to the south – *nach Süden fliegen*

Übung ▶

It is windy outside. Let's go and fly my kite!
My father always flew Swiss Air.
This silly idea flies in the face of reason.

Beachte ▶

Man darf dieses Verb nicht verwechseln mit "flow/flowed/flowed" – *fließen.*

forbid   forbade   forbidden   *verbieten*

I forbid you to meet with these horrible people again.
The law forbids driving without a licence.
My father forbade me to watch the horror video.
It is forbidden to touch the exhibits.

Idioms ▶

God forbid that ... – *Gott möge uns davor behüten, dass ...*
Heaven forbid that – *der Himmel möge uns davor bewahren*
God forbid! – *Gott bewahre!*

Übung ▶

Drinking in public is forbidden in some countries.
Lack of the time forbade us to go into more detail.
My health forbids me from travelling to France.

Hinweis ▶

forbidding – *abstoßend, widerwärtig; bedrohlich*

forecast   forecast/ed   forecast/ed   *vorhersagen*

I cannot forecast the outcome of this adventure.
The meteorologist forecast that there would be a disastrous hailstorm.
They have forecast that we will get some snow tomorrow.

Übung ▶

He couldn't forecast the coming events.
Have they forecast rain for tomorrow?
It isn't always easy to forecast the weather.

foresee foresaw foreseen   *voraussehen, absehen*

He never foresees any difficulties and afterwards he complains.
We foresaw that things would not work out well.
I could not have foreseen that he would react like that.

You could have foreseen this problem long ago – it is too late now.
I can't understand why the politicians didn't foresee the crisis.
I'm sure he didn't foresee the accident.

◀ **Übung**

foretell foretold foretold   *voraussagen*

Can you foretell my future?
Who can foretell whether our democratic system will last?
The old lady foretold that he would be saved.
It was foretold to us that the Messiah would come.

Whoever fortold that, was wrong.
Nobody can foretell what will happen tomorrow.
If I was able to foretell the future I could give you better advice.

◀ **Übung**

forget forgot forgotten   *vergessen*

He never forgets to give me a call when he arrives.
Don't forget to be there at ten o'clock!
I forgot to take the cake out of the oven.
She has forgotten her gloves on the table.

to forget a language – *eine Sprache verlernen*
to forget oneself – *sich vergessen, aus der Rolle fallen*
to forget one's differences – *seine Meinungsverschiedenheiten ruhen lassen*
Forget it! – *Vergiss es! Es ist nicht wichtig!*
Forget about it! – *Reg dich nicht auf!*
never to be forgotten – *unvergesslich*
And don't you forget it! – *Und dass du das ja nicht vergisst!*
not forgetting ... – *nicht zu vergessen ...*
You might as well forget it! – *Das kannst du vergessen!*

◀ **Idioms**

Übung

What was the film called starring Robert Redford! – Sorry, I forgot.
Don't forget yourself!
Can't you forget your differences for just one moment?

forgive forgave forgiven *vergeben, vergessen*

Please forgive me for not writing to you in such a long time.
He forgives everybody, no matter what they have done.
I was glad that he forgave me my impertinent behaviour.
Don't worry – it is all forgiven and forgotten.

Idioms

to forgive someone a debt – *jemandem eine Schuld erlassen*
forgive me, but ... – *Entschuldigung, aber ...*
to forgive and forget – *vergeben und vergessen*

Übung

She'll never forgive herself if anything happens to the children.
The bank won't forgive you your debt.
Forgive me, but you wanted to go to the theatre!

freeze froze frozen *(ge)frieren*

Every winter the lock of my car door freezes (up).
It was so cold that the milk froze in the cellar last night.
All the country roads were frozen.

Idioms

to freeze in one's tracks – *wie angewurzelt stehen bleiben*
to freeze someone to the spot – *wie angewurzelt stehen bleiben wegen etwas*
to make someone's blood freeze – *jemandes Blut in den Adern erstarren lassen (vor Angst, Schreck)*
to freeze to death – *erfrieren*
Freeze! – *Keine Bewegung!*
to freeze somebody with a look – *jemandem einen eisigen Blick zuwerfen*
to freeze off – *die kalte Schulter zeigen*

Übung

In wintertime Lake Erie is often frozen over/up.
I was freezing because I had forgotten to bring my coat.
If we have some food left over, we can freeze it.

get   got   got   *bekommen; werden*

You will get a cold if you stay out in the rain.
When I stayed in Australia, I got a lot of mail from my American friends.
She has got really exited about it.

to get something across – *etwas „rüberbringen", etwas verständlich machen*   ◄ Idioms
to get along with someone – *mit jemandem auskommen*
to get ahead – *vorankommen, Karriere machen*
to get carried away – *sich mitreißen lassen*
to get down to business – *zur Sache kommen*
to get down to something – *etwas in Angriff nehmen*
to get into a jam – *in Schwierigkeiten geraten*
to get into the habit of doing something – *sich etwas angewöhnen*
to get in touch with someone – *mit jemandem Kontakt aufnehmen, jemanden anrufen*
to get out of hand – *außer Kontrolle geraten*
to get rid of somehting/someone – *etwas/jemanden loswerden*
to get the better of someone – *die Oberhand über jemanden gewinnen, jemanden ausstechen*
to get the better of something – *etwas überwinden*
to get the hang of something – *den Dreh rauskriegen*
to get one's hooks into someone – *jemanden in seine Klauen bekommen*
to get someone's nerves – *jemandem auf die Nerven gehen*
to get going – *in Gang kommen, in Gang bringen*
to get away with something – *ungestraft davonkommen mit etwas*
to get back at someone for something – *jemandem etwas heimzahlen*
to get the sack – *entlassen werden*
to get hold of the wrong end of the stick – *etwas falsch verstehen*
to get something over with – *etwas hinter sich bringen*
How are you! – Well, I get by – *Wie geht's? – Es geht so, ich komme so zurecht*
What has got into you? – *Was ist denn in dich gefahren?*

Übung

I am not trying to criticise you. Please do not get me wrong!
I did not get that. Could you explain it once more please?
You won't get away with that!

Beachte

Im AE heißt das Past participle meist "gotten".

give gave given *geben*

If you give me your address, I can write to you.
Last year they gave a concert in Boston.
He has given up his job because of the accident.
I have just been given a lot of money by my grandmother.

Idioms

to give as good as one gets – *es jemandem mit gleicher Münze heimzahlen*
to give someone the cold shoulder – *jemandem die kalte Schulter zeigen*
to give oneself airs – *sich aufspielen, angeben*
to give in to someone – *jemandem nachgeben*
to give someone a hand with something – *jemandem bei etwas helfen*
to give evidence of something – *zeugen von etwas*
to give birth to – *gebären, zur Welt bringen*
to give vent to a feeling – *einem Gefühl Luft machen*
to give way to something – *Platz machen für etwas, ersetzt werden durch*
to give something away (a secret) – *etwas verraten, ausplaudern*
to give someone the creeps – *eine Gänsehaut bekommen, erschauern, jemanden kalt überlaufen*
Don't give me that! – *Das glaubst du doch selbst nicht!*
to give rise to – *verursachen*
I don't give a damn about it! – *Das ist mir völlig egal!*
to give someone one's love – *jemandem herzliche Grüße bestellen*
to give someone a piece of one's mind – *jemandem ordentlich die Meinung sagen*
to give a smile to someone – *jemanden anlächeln*
to give a lecture – *einen Vortrag halten*
to give the world for something – *alles geben für etwas*
to be given up for dead – *für tot gehalten werden*
to give it to someone – *es jemandem „geben" (verprügeln, die Meinung sagen)*

After we had tried to find him for four days, we gave up all hope.
Imagine, I have finally given up smoking!
He gave me his word not to tell anybody.

go   went   gone   *gehen (fahren, reisen)*

Do you go shopping every day?
This motorway goes to Edinburgh.
We went to London by train.
I went to school in Canada, but I studied in the United States.
Prices have gone down noticeably.

to go about something – *etwas angehen, handhaben*
to go awry – *schief gehen (Sache); sich irren (Person)*
to go by appearances – *nach dem Aussehen urteilen*
to go down to the country – *aufs Land fahren, gehen (weg von der Stadt)*
to go Dutch – *die Kosten teilen*
to go for a walk – *spazieren gehen*
to go in one ear and out the other – *zum einen Ohr hinein, zum anderen hinaus gehen*
to go to great trouble/lengths to do something – *sich bei etwas besondere Mühe geben*
to go out of one's way to do something – *sich ganz besonders anstrengen etwas zu tun*
to go to the dogs – *vor die Hunde gehen*
to go along with someone – *mit jemandem übereinstimmen*
to go in for something – *sich für etwas interessieren, sich mit etwas befassen*
to go on and on about something – *nicht aufhören, über etwas zu reden*
to go off the beaten track – *etwas Ungewöhnliches tun*
to go out of fashion – *aus der Mode kommen*
to go with the times – *mit der Zeit gehen*
to go too far – *zu weit gehen*
to go in history – *in die Geschichte eingehen*
There you go! – *Na also!*
That goes for all of you. – *Das gilt für euch alle.*
That goes without saying. – *Das versteht sich von selbst.*
Anything goes. – *Alles ist erlaubt, möglich.*

Übung

I am sorry, but I must be going.
My car is gone. Someone must have stolen it.
I cannot go into details for reasons of time.
If you really want to do that, go for it!
Do you mind if I switch on the radio? – Go ahead!

grind   ground   ground   *mahlen*

Do you buy ground coffee or do you grind the coffee beans at home?
A few years ago we always ground the coffee beans ourselves.
Wheat is ground down into flour in a mill.

Idioms

to grind one's teeth – *mit den Zähnen knirschen*
to grind something into someone – *jemandem etwas eintrichtern, einhämmern*
to grind for something – *pauken, büffeln für etwas (z.B. Prüfung)*
to grind someone down – *jemanden unterdrücken, schinden*
to grind to a halt – *zum Erliegen kommen, zum Stillstand kommen*
to have an axe to grind – *eigennützige Ziele verfolgen*
to grind something to a powder – *etwas fein zermahlen/zerstoßen*
to grind one's heel into the earth – *den Absatz in die Erde bohren*
to grind away – *schuften*
to grind towards something – *einer Sache unaufhaltsam entgegengehen*
to grind up – *zermahlen*

Übung

This knife does not cut. It needs to be ground.
Would you please grind the dried herbs into a powder?
The miller was grinding corn all day.

grow   grew   grown   *wachsen*

In our garden grows a huge tree.
I grew up in California, but I live in Italy now.
How tall you have grown since I last saw you!
Our school has grown rapidly over the last five years.

to grow old/dark – *alt/dunkel werden*
to grow apart – *sich auseinander entwicklen, sich auseinander leben*
to grow away from someone – *sich jemandem entfremden*
to grow in numbers – *zahlreicher werden*
to grow in wisdom – *weiser werden*
to grow into someone – *sich entwickeln zu, heranwachsen zu*
to grow into something – *in etwas hineinwachsen (Arbeit)*
to grow out of something – *aus etwas herauswachsen; zu alt für etwas werden*
to grow out of a habit – *eine Gewohnheit ablegen*
to grow together – *zusammenwachsen, sich besser verstehen*
something grows on someone – *sich immer mehr an etwas gewöhnen; jemandem ans Herz wachsen*
to grow a beard – *sich einen Bart wachsen lassen*
to grow to hate somebody – *jemanden hassen lernen*
to grow used to something – *sich an etwas gewöhnen*
to grow like somebody – *jemandem immer ähnlicher werden*
to grow a woman – *zur Frau heranwachsen*
to grow a crisis – *sich zur Krise auswachsen*
to grow out of a habit – *eine Angewohnheit ablegen*
Grow up! – *Werde endlich erwachsen!*
Money doesn't grow on trees. – *Geld fällt nicht vom Himmel.*

◄ Idioms

My family grows potatoes in the garden.
Last year I grew my hair long for the first time.
When I am grown up, I want to be a pilot.

◄ Übung

hang hung hung   *hängen*

My mother hangs the washing out in the garden.
An expensive picture hung on his wall.
Big red apples hung from the branches of the tree.
I have hung photographs of my family on the wall.

to hang around/about – *"herumhängen", herumlungern, dableiben*
to hang by a (single) thread – *an einem seidenen Faden hängen*
to hang on someone's lips – *an jemandes Lippen hängen*

◄ Idioms

to let something go hang – *etwas vernachlässigen*
to hang onto something – *sich festhalten an, sich halten an etwas*
to hang wallpaper – *tapezieren*
to hang clothes on the line – *Wäsche aufhängen*
to hang one's head – *den Kopf hängenlassen*
to hang oneself – *sich erhängen*
(I'm) hanged if I will – *den Teufel werd ich ...*
to hang in the air – *in der Schwebe sein*
to be sentenced to hang – *zum Tode durch Erhängen verurteilt werden*
to hang behind – *zurückbleiben; herumtrödeln*
Hang tight, we're off! – *Festhalten, es geht los!*
Hang on! – *Bleib' dran, einen Augenblick, warte mal! (besonders am Telefon), Halt! Moment!*
Hang it all! – *Verflixt! Mist!*
Hang him! – *Zum Kuckuck mit ihm!*

Übung ▶

He got so angry that he hung up on me.
He didn't pass the exam. That's why he hung himself.
They always hang behind when we go for a walk.

Beachte ▶

> "hang" wird regelmäßig gebildet bei:
> The murderer was hanged – *Der Mörder wurde gehängt.*

have had had *haben*

Have you got/Do you have a pencil that I can borrow?
Suddenly I had a splendid idea.
We have had fish and chips for dinner.

Idioms ▶

to have a go at something – *etwas ausprobieren, versuchen*
to have a try at something – *einen Versuch machen mit etwas*
to have a good command of something – *etwas beherrschen, gut können*
to have a bone to pick with someone – *mit jemandem ein Hühnchen zu rupfen haben*
to have a crush on someone – *in jemanden verknallt sein*
to have a grudge against someone – *jemanden vergrollen*
to have a liking for someone – *jemanden gern mögen, eine Vorliebe haben für jemanden*

to have a say in something – *bei etwas mitzureden haben*
to have a word with someone – *kurz mit jemandem sprechen*
to have words with someone – *sich mit jemandem streiten*
to have what it takes – *das gewisse Etwas haben, das Zeug haben zu*
to have someone on – *jemanden zum Besten haben*
to have one's tongue in one's cheek – *etwas ironisch meinen, zum Spass sagen, auf den Arm nehmen*
to have one's heart in one's mouth – *zu Tode erschrocken sein*
to have a finger in every pie – *überall mitmischen*
to have something at one's fingertips – *etwas parat haben; etwas gut beherrschen*
to have one's way – *seinen Willen/Kopf durchsetzen*
to have the time of one's life – *einen Riesenspaß haben*
to have it out with someone – *etwas bereinigen mit jemandem, etwas in Ordnung bringen mit, klarstellen*
to have something up one's sleeves – *eine Überraschung parat haben*
to have many irons in the fire – *viele Eisen im Feuer haben*
to have pity on someone – *jemanden bemitleiden*
I had better do it. – *Ich sollte es besser tun, es wäre besser, wenn ich es täte.*

Please have a sandwich! ◄ **Übung**
Let me have a look!
He had a weakness for beautiful women.

> Das Verb "have" wird natürlich auch als Hilfsverb gebraucht! ◄ **Beachte**

hear   hard   heard   *hören*

My grandfather is deaf – he cannot hear anything at all.
He heard someone entering the house.
Have you heard this piece of music before?
I have heard that Australia is a fascinating country.

to hear someone out – *jemanden ausreden lassen* ◄ **Idioms**
to hear from someone – *Nachrichten erhalten von jemandem*
to hear about something – *etwas erfahren*

to make oneself heard – *sich Gehör verschaffen*
I must be hearing things. – *Ich glaube, ich höre nicht richtig.*
to hear a case – *einen Fall verhandeln*
to hear evidence – *Zeugen vernehmen*
Lord, hear us. – *Herr, erhöre uns.*
Hear, hear! – *Hört, hört!; Sehr richtig!*
we would not hear of it – *wir wollten nichts davon wissen*

Übung

I hope to hear from you soon!
It was so quiet that one could hear a pin drop.
No, I have never heard of such a book.
Since my friend Lucy went to Australia I have not heard of her.

hide   hid   hidden   *(sich) verstecken*

I always hide behind the door to frighten my little sister.
My mother hid the money from the thieves under the carpet.
We could not see the house because it was hidden behind some trees.

Idioms

to hide one's feelings – *seine Gefühle verbergen*
to hide out – *sich verstecken*

Übung

I can tell you everything. I have nothing to hide.
This afternoon my dog has hidden my car keys.
She's not able to hide her feelings.

Hinweis

hide-and-seek – *Versteckspiel*

hit   hit   hit   *schlagen; treffen*

I always hit the target.
The tennis player hit the ball across the court.
I slipped and hit my head against the wall.
She hit the boy with her car.

Idioms

to hit the nail on the head – *den Nagel auf den Kopf treffen*
to hit it off with someone – *mit jemandem schnell warm werden, sich gut verstehen mit jemandem*

You have hit it! – *Du hast es richtig getroffen, erraten; So ist es! Genau!*

to hit the ceiling/roof – *vor Wut in die Luft gehen*

to hit the jackpot – *das große Los ziehen, Glück haben*

to hit the road – *abreisen, aufbrechen, sich auf den Weg machen*

to hit back someone – *zurückschlagen, sich verteidigen, einen Gegenschlag unternehmen, jemandem Kontra geben*

to hit someone a blow – *jemandem einen Schlag versetzen*

to hit the hay – *sich in die Falle hauen*

to hit the head against something – *sich den Kopf an etwas anstoßen*

to hit one's way out of trouble – *sich freischlagen; sich freiboxen*

to be hard hit by something – *von etwas schwer getroffen werden*

to hit the papers – *in die Zeitungen kommen*

to hit town – *die Stadt erreichen*

to hit a problem – *auf ein Problem stoßen*

to hit the roof – *an die Decke gehen*

to hit the bottle – *zur Flasche greifen*

to hit the dance floor – *tanzen*

to hit out at somebody – *jemanden scharf angreifen*

I've been hit! – *Mich hat's erwischt!*

You've hit it on the head! – *Du hast es genau getroffen!*

When she crossed the road, she was hit by a car.
My mother's sudden death has hit my father hard.
When we dug deeper, we hit water.

◄ **Übung**

a hit-and-run offence – *Fahrerflucht*   ◄ **Hinweis**

hold **held held**   *halten*

Could you hold my gloves for a second?
She held a newspaper in her hand.
The crowd was held back by the police.

to hold someone/something at bay – *jemanden in Schach halten; etwas unter Kontrolle haben*   ◄ **Idioms**

to hold one's nose/ears – *sich die Nase/Ohren zuhalten*
to hold one's tongue – *den Mund halten*
to hold a meeting – *eine Versammlung abhalten*
to hold elections – *Wahlen abhalten*
to hold one's ground – *sich behaupten*
to hold on to something – *festhalten an etwas*
to hold one's breath – *den Atem anhalten*
to hold someone in high/low esteem/regard – *jemanden hoch schätzen, hoch achten*
to hold something cheap – *eine niedrige Meinung von etwas haben*
to hold someone responsible for something – *jemanden verantwortlich machen für*
to hold something against someone – *jemandem etwas vorhalten, vorwerfen; jemandem etwas übel nehmen*
to hold with something – *etwas billigen, einverstanden sein mit etwas*
to hold one's own with someone – *neben jemandem bestehen können, sich behaupten gegen*
to hold something back – *etwas verschweigen, vorenthalten*
to hold true for – *zutreffen auf, gelten für*
to hold the view that – *der Ansicht sein, dass*
to hold someone dear – *jemanden lieb haben*
not hold water – *nicht stichhaltig sein*
Hold the line! – *Bitte bleiben Sie am Apparat!*
Hold on a minute! – *Warte mal! Moment mal! (vgl. Hang on!)*
Hold it! – *Halt! Stopp!*

Übung ▶

They were so much in love that they held hands all the time.
I hope this bad weather does not hold for long.
She thinks he's holding something back.

hurt   hurt   hurt   *(sich) verletzen, wehtun*

It hurts when you pull my hair.
I fell down the stairs and hurt my foot.
He was badly hurt in the war.
I hope you have not hurt yourself.
Nothing hurts like the truth.

Idioms ▶

to hurt someone's feelings – *jemandes Gefühle verletzen, jemanden kränken*

to hurt oneself – *sich wehtun*
that won't hurt – *es schadet nichts, wird schon nichts schaden*
He would not hurt a fly. – *Er würde keiner Fliege etwas zuleide tun.*

I was deeply hurt by his criticism.
The doctor asked: Where does it hurt?
It never hurts to talk to somebody.

keep   kept   kept   *(be)halten; aufbewahren*

You can keep the pen if you like. I don't need it.
My sister keeps all the photographs of her ex-boy-friend.
Many years ago we kept a dog.
I have kept the keys for him while he has been away.

to keep something – *dranbleiben an einer Arbeit, weitermachen mit etwas*
to keep up with someone – *mit jemandem mithalten*
to keep one's fingers crossed – *die Daumen drücken*
to keep one's pecker up – *den Mut nicht sinken lassen, die Ohren steif halten*
to keep an eye on something – *ein Auge auf etwas haben, etwas im Auge behalten*
to keep someone at arm's length – *jemanden auf Distanz halten*
to keep someone at bay – *jemanden in Schach halten*
to keep something in mind – *etwas nicht vergessen, an etwas denken (vgl. to bear something in mind)*
to keep in touch with someone – *in Kontakt bleiben mit jemandem*
to keep on doing something – *etwas weiterhin tun, fortfahren, etwas zu tun*
to keep quiet – *ruhig bleiben, sich ruhig verhalten*
to keep someone company – *jemandem Gesellschaft leisten*
to keep track of something – *etwas verfolgen, sich auf dem Laufenden halten über*
to keep a record of something – *Buch führen über etwas*
to keep out of sight – *sich nicht blicken lassen*
to keep someone from doing something – *jemanden davon abhalten, etwas zu tun*

to keep up appearances – *den Schein wahren*
to keep someone waiting – *jemanden warten lassen*
to keep someone in dark about something – *jemanden über etwas im Ungewissen lassen*
to keep cool – *gelassen bleiben*
to keep clear of something – *sich fern halten von etwas*
to keep fit – *fit, in Form bleiben*
to keep someone in his place – *jemanden in seine Schranken weisen*
I won't keep you long. – *Ich werde dich nicht lange aufhalten.*
Keep it up! – *Weiter so!*
Keep your chin up! – *Halt die Ohren steif!*

Übung ▶

Please keep your seat!
I will tell you about it if you can keep a secret.
She was very unreliable. She never kept her promises.
Keep off the grass!

know   knew   known   *kennen; wissen*

Do you know this man?
I knew that he would blame me for it.
They have known each other since they were children.
She once knew a boy from China.

Idioms ▶

to know something by heart – *etwas auswendig können*
to know something inside out – *etwas in- und auswendig kennen*
to be in the know – *Bescheid wissen, sich auskennen*
to know two people apart – *auseinander halten können*
to know on which side one's bread is buttered – *auf seinen Vorteil aus sein, sich beliebt machen*
to know one's mind – *wissen, was man will*
to know somebody by his walk – *jemanden am Gang erkennen*
to get to know somebody – *jemanden kennen lernen*
to let somebody know something – *jemanden etwas wissen lassen*
not that I know of – *nicht, dass ich wüsste*
as far as I know – *so viel ich weiß*
you never know – *man kann nie wissen*
there's no knowing – *das kann keiner sagen*

it is well known that ... – *es ist allgemein bekannt, dass ...*
to make it known that ... – *bekannt geben, dass ...*
to become known – *berühmt werden*
I don't know about that! – *Da bin ich mir nicht so sicher!*
I know all about you! – *Ich weiß über Sie Bescheid!*

Do you know how to play tennis?
He is known as a terrible liar.
I knew her by her voice.

lay   laid   laid   *legen*

Hens lay eggs.
I laid my bag on the seat.
We have laid the carpet in our living-room ourselves.

to lay the table – *den Tisch decken*
to lay one's cards on the table – *die Karten auf den Tisch legen*
to lay stress on something – *etwas betonen, hervorheben*
to lay claim to something – *Anspruch erheben auf etwas*
to lay it on a bit thick – *etwas zu dick auftragen, übertreiben*
to lay the blame for something on someone – *jemandem die Schuld für etwas zuschieben*
to lay hand on something – *etwas in die Finger bekommen, erwischen*
to lay plans – *Pläne machen*
to lay a hand on somebody – *jemandem etwas tun; Hand an jemanden legen*
to lay a trap for somebody – *jemandem eine Falle stellen*
to lay responsibility for something on somebody – *jemanden für etwas verantwortlich machen*
to lay waste – *verwüsten*
to lay somebody away – *jemanden zu Grabe tragen*
to lay something before somebody – *jemandem etwas vorlegen*
to lay one's arms – *die Waffen niederlegen*
to lay one's life – *sein Leben opfern*
to lay a tax on something – *etwas besteuern*

You can lay the coat on my sofa if you like.
He laid a trap to catch the mouse.
Don't you think you're laying it on a bit thick?

lead led led   *führen, leiten*

This road leads to London.
He led the choir quite successfully.
We were led through the city by an experienced guide.

Idioms ▶

to lead the way – *den Weg zeigen, vorangehen*
to lead someone astray – *auf den falschen Weg führen*
to lead someone on – *jemanden auf den Arm nehmen*
to lead someone up the garden path – *jemanden an der Nase herumführen*
to lead up to – *führen zu*
to lead a government – *an der Regierungsspitze stehen*
to lead a party – *Parteivorsitzender sein*
to lead a life of luxury – *ein Luxusleben führen*
to lead somebody to do something – *jemanden dazu bringen etwas zu tun*
to lead a witness – *einen Zeugen/eine Zeugin beeinflussen*
to lead somebody to believe that ... – *jemandem den Eindruck vermitteln, dass ...*
to lead somebody into trouble – *jemanden in Schwierigkeiten bringen*
to lead aside – *beiseite nehmen*
to lead on – *anführen*

Übung ▶

I wonder what this will lead to.
She led me to believe that she was a famous actress.
He led a dog's life while he was in China.
I never knew that he led a double life.

lean leant/leaned leant/leaned   *(sich)lehnen*

You can lean your bike against the wall.
She leant out of the window too far and fell to the ground.
He has leant back in the chair.

Idioms ▶

to lean over backwards to do something – *sich die größte Mühe geben, etwas zu tun*
to lean towards – *tendieren zu, eine Tendenz zeigen zu*
to lean on someone/something – *abhängig sein von, sich stützen auf, sich verlassen auf, bauen auf*
to lean over – *sich bücken*
to lean on somebody – *jemanden bearbeiten*

I leant forward to be able to see her.
She is leaning upon her elbows.
My sister always leant on her husband.

◀ Übung

the leaning tower of Pisa – *der Schiefe Turm von Pisa*

◀ Hinweis

leap leapt/leaped leapt/leaped *springen*

A horse leaps over a fence without difficulty.
Suddenly she leapt into the cold water.
We have leant up from the sofa because you have entered.

◀ Idioms

to leap a chance – *die Gelegenheit sofort wahrnehmen*
to leap at an offer – *sich auf ein Angebot stürzen*
to leap to the eye – *ins Auge springen*
to leap out at someone – *jemandem ins Auge springen, hervorstechen*
to leap in one's mind – *jemandem schlagartig in den Sinn kommen*
to leap a wall – *über eine Wand springen*
to leap at conclusions – *voreilige Schlüsse ziehen*
to be ready to leap and strike – *sprungbereit sein*
to make hearts leap for joy – *die Herzen höher schlagen lassen*
to leap to one's feet – *aufspringen*
to leap up into the air – *in die Luft springen*
Look before you leap! – *Erst denken, dann handeln!*

◀ Übung

I was scared when the big dog leapt up at me.
The horse leapt over the wall.
Don't leap to conclusions!

◀ Hinweis

leap-year – *Schaltjahr*

learn learnt/learned learnt/learned *lernen; erfahren*

It is a good idea to learn English.
He is a clever boy – he learns very fast.
I learnt how to play the piano.
We have learnt to live with our problems.
We were really shocked when we learnt of/about the accident.

Idioms ▶

to learn something by heart – *etwas auswendig lernen*
to learn something the hard way – *etwas aus bitterer Erfahrung lernen*
to learn one's lesson – *einen Denkzettel bekommen, seine Lektion erteilt bekommen*
you live and learn – *man lernt nie aus*
to learn from experience – *aus Erfahrung lernen*
to learn up – *(auswendig) lernen*

Übung ▶

I have just learnt that his mother is in hospital.
Fortunately, he has learnt from his mistakes.
We have to learn this poem by heart.

leave left left *(ver)lassen*

When will you leave New York?
My aunt left her husband for a younger man.
We left from the airport early in the morning.
I have left a message for you on the kitchen table.
John is not here anymore. He left for work at 7.00 this morning.

Idioms ▶

to leave no stone unturned – *alle Hebel in Bewegung setzen, nichts unversucht lassen*
to leave someone alone – *jemanden in Ruhe lassen*
to leave a lot to be desired – *viel zu wünschen übrig lassen*
to leave someone in the lurch – *jemanden im Stich lassen*
to leave someone cold – *jemanden kalt lassen, nicht interessieren, gelassen hinnehmen*
to leave it at that – *es dabei belassen, bewenden lassen*
to leave something to chance – *etwas dem Zufall überlassen*
to be left out in the cold – *ignoriert werden, übergangen werden*
to be left (over) – *übrig sein*
to leave for Edinburgh – *nach Edinburgh aufbrechen*
to be left until called for – *postlagernd*
to leave school – *von der Schule abgehen*
to leave the table – *vom Tisch aufstehen*
to leave the road – *von der Straße abkommen*
to leave somebody to himself – *jemanden alleine lassen*
to leave something to the last minute – *mit etwas bis zur letzten Minute warten*

to leave something to chance – *etwas dem Zufall überlassen*
to leave nothing to accident – *nichts dem Zufall überlassen*
leaving aside the fact that ... – *wenn man die Tatsache außer Acht lässt, dass ...*
to feel left out – *sich ausgeschlossen fühlen*
Leave me alone! – *Lass mich in Ruhe!*
Let's leave it at that. – *Lassen wir es dabei bewenden.*
Would you leave us, please? – *Würden Sie uns bitte allein lassen?*

Do not leave the window open at night.
Unfortunately, I left out seven words in the translation test.
Why don't you leave it to chance? So you don't have to make a decision now.

lend   lent   lent   *(ver)leihen*

I will lend you the money if you promise to give it back.
He lent me his car for the trip.
She has lent all her dresses to her girl-friend.

to lend someone a hand with something – *jemandem zur Hand gehen bei etwas*
to lend one's aid – *Hilfe leisten*
to lend oneself to something – *sich hergeben zu etwas*
to lend itself to something – *sich eignen für etwas*
to lend an ear to someone – *jemandem Gehör schenken*
to lend support to somebody – *jemanden unterstützen*
to lend out – *verleihen*

He asked me if he could borrow my bicycle, but I did not
want to lend it to him.
This new lamp lends the room a cosy atmosphere.
Could you please lend me a hand with this box?

let   let   let   *lassen*

Let's go to the football match.
Let me see the letter.
We always let him do what he wanted.
Why hasn't she let me wear her dress?

Idioms ▶

to let a room – *ein Zimmer vermieten*
to let the cat out of the back – *die Katze aus dem Sack lassen*
to let alone – *geschweige denn*
to let drop a remark – *eine Bemerkung fallen lassen*
to let off steam – *Dampf ablassen, explodieren*
to let oneself go – *sich gehen lassen; aus sich herausgehen*
to let oneself in for something – *sich etwas einbrocken, sich einlassen auf*
to let one's hair down – *aus sich herausgehen, sich ungezwungen benehmen, sich austoben*
to let go of something – *etwas loslassen*
to let someone down – *jemanden im Stich lassen; enttäuschen*
to let someone into a secret – *jemanden in ein Geheimnis einweihen*
to let someone off – *jemanden laufen lassen, davonkommen lassen*
to let something slip – *jemandem rutscht etwas unabsichtlich heraus, sich verplappern*
to let an opportunity slip – *sich eine Gelegenheit entgehen lassen*
to let on that ... – *verraten, dass ...*
let me see... – *mal sehen, ich muss mal überlegen ...*

Übung ▶

Please let me know when you will be arriving.
I have just seen that she has let a stranger into the house.
Why have you locked the door? Let me out at once!

lie lay (lain)   *liegen*

London lies on the River Thames.
She felt sick and had to lie down on the bed.
I lay on the beach seven days in a row.
Several cigarettes stubs lay on the floor.
The snow lay thick on the branches of the tree.

Idioms ▶

to lie heavily on someone – *schwer auf jemandem lasten*
to lie in – *morgens lange im Bett bleiben*
to lie back in an arm-chair – *sich in einem Sessel zurücklehnen*
to lie in ambush (for something) – *im Hinterhalt liegen*

to lie in ruins – *in Trümmern liegen*
to lie low – *sich versteckt halten*
to lie under an obligation – *eine Verpflichtung haben*
to lie in store for someone – *jemanden erwarten, jemandem bevorstehen*
to lie at someone's door – *liegen bei (Schuld)*
to see how the land lies – *schauen, wie die Dinge liegen; schauen, wie es steht*
to know where one's interest lies – *wissen, wo sein Vorteil liegt*
Let sleeping dogs lie. – *Schlafende Hunde soll man nicht wecken.*
it lies with you to do it – *es liegt bei dir, es zu tun; es ist deine Sache, es zu tun*
the responsibility lies with you – *die Verantwortung liegt bei dir*
as far as lies with me – *soweit es in meinen Kräften steht*

◀ **Übung**

Don't be so pessimistic! Life still lies before you.
I am sorry, but it does not lie in my power to help you.
Why are you still lying in bed? Shouldn't you go to work?

◀ **Beachte**

> Dieses Verb darf man nicht verwechseln mit:
> "lie/lied/lied" – *lügen;*
> "lay/laid/laid" – *legen (s. Seite 53)*

light lit/lighted   *anzünden; beleuchten*

Do you use a match or a lighter to light your cigarettes?
I will light the stairs so that you won't fall.
She lit a candle and entered the cave.
We have just lit a fire to warm our cold hands.

◀ **Idioms**

to light upon something – *landen auf etwas; etwas durch Zufall entdecken*
to be lit up – *angeheitert sein, beschwipst sein*
to light the way for somebody – *jemandem leuchten; jemandem den Weg weisen*
to light up – *aufleuchten; sich erhellen*

◀ **Übung**

His eyes lit up when he heard her voice.
The room was lit up by ten different lamps.
He had trouble lighting his cigarette.

lose   lost   lost   *verlieren*

I easily lose my patience.
Nobody can understand that we lost the match.
My grandfather lost an arm in the war.
I cannot enter the flat because I have lost my keys.

Idioms ▶

to lose one's head – *den Kopf verlieren*
to lose the thread (of one's argument) – *den Faden verlieren*
to lose one's mind – *verrückt werden*
to lose one's temper – *die Geduld verlieren, wütend werden*
to lose heart – *den Mut verlieren*
to lose one's heart to something/someone – *sich verlieben in etwas/jemanden*
to lose sight of something – *etwas aus den Augen verlieren*
to lose track of something – *nicht folgen können, nicht mitkommen*
to lose touch with someone – *den Kontakt mit jemandem verlieren*
to lose one's way – *sich verirren*
to lose oneself in a book – *sich in ein Buch vertiefen*
to be lost in thought – *in Gedanken verloren sein*
to lose no time in doing something – *etwas sofort tun*
to lose no opportunity to do something – *keine Gelegenheit verpassen etwas zu tun*
to get lost – *sich verlaufen; sich verirren; verloren gehen*
to lose out to somebody – *von jemandem verdrängt werden*
Get lost! – *Verschwinde!*
not lose much sleep over/about something – *sich nicht viele Sorgen über etwas machen*

We would get completely lost in this city without a map.
She seems to have lost her self-confidence.
I have lost a lot of weight during the last weeks.

make   made   made   *machen, tun*

I will make a cake for your birthday.
Every time my brother makes tea, it is terribly strong.

Did you make that dress yourself?
It made me angry to see that he beat his children.
This machine was made in the USA.

◄ **Idioms**

to make someone do something – *jemanden veranlassen etwas zu tun; jemanden etwas tun lassen*
to make both ends meet – *über die Runden kommen, sich nach der Decke strecken*
to make a deal with someone – *ein Abkommen treffen mit jemandem*
to make a fuss about something – *viel Aufhebens um etwas machen*
to make a mountain out of a molehill – *aus einer Mücke einen Elefanten machen*
to make eyes at someone – *jemandem schöne Augen machen*
to make do with something – *sich mit etwas behelfen*
to make friends with someone – *sich anfreuden mit*
to make something up – *etwas erfinden, sich etwas ausdenken*
to make up for something – *etwas wieder gutmachen*
to make it – *etwas schaffen; es schaffen, zu kommen*
to make the best of it – *das Beste aus etwas machen*
to make the most of it – *etwas in vollen Zügen genießen, etwas (eine Gelegenheit) ausnützen*
to make up one's mind – *sich entschließen, eine Entscheidung zu treffen*
to be unable to make head or tail of something – *aus etwas nicht schlau werden, sich keinen Reim machen können*
to make someone's hair stand on end – *jemandem die Haare zu Berge stehen lassen*
to make a point of something – *Wert auf etwas legen; sich etwas zum Prinzip machen*
to make for the door – *auf die Tür zusteuern, zueilen*
to make a sense of something – *etwas verstehen, begreifen*
Make yourself at home! – *Fühl dich wie zu Hause, mach es dir bequem!*

◄ **Übung**

Have you heard the President's speech? What do you make of it?
My new boy-friend has made a bad impression on my mother.
I will make sure that you get an invitation, too.
Their new house is made of wood.

mean meant meant — *meinen; bedeuten*

I do not know what you mean by that.
What does dyslexia mean?
This traffic sign means that you must not turn left.
Believe me, I meant what I said.
Did you understand what was meant by that sentence?
It meant a lot to him that she called on his birthday.

Idioms

to mean to do something – *beabsichtigen etwas zu tun; etwas tun wollen*
to mean well – *es gut meinen*
not mean harm – *es nicht böse meinen*
to mean business – *es ernst meinen*
to be meant for somebody – *für jemanden bestimmt sein*
to mean somebody to do something – *wollen, dass jemand etwas tut*
I mean it! – *Das ist mein Ernst!*

Übung

They were meant for each other.
Is this letter meant to be an "a" or an "o"?
Don't be afraid. He means well.

meet met met — *begegnen, treffen*

Our chess club meets every Sunday evening.
These two roads meet after two miles.
We met at a party and fell in love immediately.
On my journey to India I met a great number of very interesting people.
What a surprise! I have just met an old friend of mine.

Idioms

to meet a difficulty – *mit einer Schwierigkeit fertig werden*
to meet someone's expectations – *jemandes Erwartungen entsprechen*
to meet with an accident – *einen Unfall erleiden, haben*
to meet with success – *Erfolg haben*
to meet with approval – *Beifall finden*
to meet with a refusal – *auf Ablehnung stoßen*
to meet one's fate – *seinem Schicksal begegnen*
to meet one's end – *sterben*
to meet someone's eye – *den Blick erwidern*
to meet up with someone – *jemanden (zufällig) treffen*

to meet death calmly – *dem Tod gefasst entgegentreten*
to meet a challenge – *sich einer Herausforderung stellen*
to meet halfway – *einen Kompromiss schließen*
to meet with derision – *verspottet werden*
to meet a warm welcome – *herzlich empfangen werden*
to arrange to meet somebody – *sich mit jemandem verabreden*

Nice (Pleased) to meet you!
I will meet you at the station at half past seven.
Yesterday I met up with an old friend from school.

pay   paid   paid   *(be)zahlen*

I can only lend you the money if you pay me back by Friday.
In Switzerland people pay fewer taxes than in Germany.
We paid only twenty pounds for our television set.
This car is already paid for. You need not give me any money for it.
At least he always paid his debts.
We get paid at the end of the month.
I have not paid my bills yet.

to pay attention to something/someone – *etwas/jemandem aufmerksam zuhören*
to pay heed to something/someone – *achten auf etwas, etwas Beachtung schenken*
to pay someone back – *es jemandem heimzahlen*
to pay someone a visit – *jemanden besuchen*
to pay someone a compliment on something – *jemandem ein Kompliment machen*
to pay homage to someone – *jemandem huldigen, Anerkennung zollen*
to pay through the nose for something (sl) – *ganz schön zahlen bei etwas, kräftig zahlen müssen, viel zu viel zahlen müssen*
to pay one's way – *ohne Verlust arbeiten, sich selbst tragen (Geschäft, Firma)*
to pay dearly for something – *teuer zu stehen kommen, schwer für etwas bezahlen müssen*
to pay off – *erfolgreich sein, sich lohnen*
to pay for itself – *sich amortisieren*
to pay shareholders – *Dividenden ausschütten*

to pay a visit on somebody – *jemandem einen Besuch abstatten*
to pay on account – *auf Rechnung zahlen*
You'll pay for that! – *Das wirst du mir büßen!*

I did not have any money at all. I could not even pay the newsboy.
It does not pay to steal.
Are you paying cash or by cheque?
I have paid all the money I have into my bank account.
One day we will have to pay for our sins.
Finally my parents have paid off the house – now they are free of debt.

put   put   put   *setzen, stellen, legen*

Put your feet on the table if you like.
He put the vacuum cleaner in the corner.
I have never put sugar in my coffee in my whole life.
I have put the meat in the refrigerator.

to put an end to something – *etwas ein Ende bereiten, Schluss machen mit etwas*
to put someone in his place – *jemanden in seine Schranken weisen*
to put into words – *in Worte fassen*
to put on weight – *zunehmen (Gewicht)*
to put one's foot in it – *ins Fettnäpfchen treten*
to put one's foot down – *ein Machtwort sprechen, energisch werden, einschreiten*
to put the lid on something – *einer Sache die Krone aufsetzen, dem Fass den Boden ausschlagen*
to put the screws on someone – *Druck auf jemanden ausüben*
to put something right – *etwas richtig stellen*
to put something up – *jemanden beherbergen, im Haus aufnehmen als Gast*
to put the blame for something on someone – *jemandem die Schuld für etwas Geben*
to put the cart before the horse – *das Pferd von hinten aufzäumen*
to put up with something – *sich etwas gefallen lassen, sich abfinden mit etwas*

to put a spoke in someone's wheel – *jemandem einen Knüppel zwischen die Beine werfen, Hindernisse in den Weg legen*
to put in an appearance – *erscheinen, auftauchen*
not put it past someone – *jemandem etwas (durchaus) zutrauen (in negativem Sinne)*
to put an animal away – *ein Tier einschläfern*
to put one's mind to something – *sich mit etwas befassen, sich etwas widmen*
to put into action/practice – *in die Tat umsetzen*
to put someone to shame – *jemanden beschämen (übertreffen)*
to put something off – *etwas aufschieben, verschieben*
to be put off by something – *abgestoßen sein von etwas*
to put on an act – *Theater spielen, sich verstellen*
to put something to someone – *jemanden informieren, jemandem etwas unterbreiten, vorschlagen*
to put all one's eggs in one basket – *alles auf eine Karte setzen*
to put oneself in someone else's shoes – *sich in einen anderen hineinversetzen*

to put it in another way ...
I don't know how to put it ...
to put it in a nutshell ...
If you want to register for this course, you must put your name down on this list.
We are leaving. Put on your coat and come along!
At the youth hostel the lights were always put out at 11 p.m.

read read read   *lesen*

Can you read her hand-writing?
When I was five years old, I could read but not write yet.
Please read this passage aloud that we can all hear it.
My grandmother read us fairy-tales when we were little.
I read about the accident in the paper.
I have just read an article on Chinese food.

to read between the lines – *zwischen den Zeilen lesen*
to read someone like a book – *jemanden sehr gut kennen; wissen, was jemand denkt*

to read a subject at University – *ein Fach studieren*
to read on – *weiterlesen*
to read something out – *etwas laut vorlesen*
to read up on something – *nachlesen über etwas*
to take it as read that ... – *davon ausgehen können, dass ...*
to be well-read in something – *belesen sein in etwas, viel wissen über etwas*
to read music – *Noten lesen*
to read somebody's palm – *jemandem aus der Hand lesen*
to read the tea leaves – *aus dem Kaffeesatz lesen*
to read a meter – *einen Zählerstand ablesen*
to read to oneself – *für sich lesen*
Read my lips! – *Höre meine Worte!*
Do you read me? – *Können Sie mich verstehen? Haben Sie mich verstanden?*

Übung

I knew him so well that I could read his thoughts.
He reads the map while I drive.
I can play the guitar although I cannot read music.
I can recommend this book. It reads very well.

ride   rode   ridden   *reiten, fahren*

Can you ride a horse?
When we lived in the country, we always rode our horses to school.
He rode his bicycle up the hill.
I have never ridden on an elephant in my whole life.

Idioms

to ride one's hobby-horse – *seinem Steckenpferd nachgehen*
to ride again – *wieder da sein*
to ride on air – *selig sein vor Glück, wie auf Wolken schweben*
to ride for a fall – *eine riskante Sache machen*
to ride high – *ganz oben sein, viel Erfolg haben*
to let something ride – *die Dinge ihren Lauf nehmen lassen*
to ride roughshod over something – *rücksichtslos über etwas hinweggehen*
to ride someone on one's shoulders – *jemanden auf den Schultern tragen*
to ride up – *hochrutschen, verrutschen (z.B. Rock)*
to be ridden by fears – *angstgepeinigt sein*

to ride at anchor – *vor Anker liegen*
to ride two horses at the same time – *auf zwei Hochzeiten tanzen*
to ride the waves – *auf den Wellen treiben*
to ride an argument to death – *ein Argument totreden*
to ride behind – *hinten sitzen; hinterherreiten; hinterherfahren*

He rode away in a hurry.
We rode home from school on a bus.
Look at him! He must be ridden by the devil!

ring   rang   rung   *läuten*

In our office the telephone rings all the time.
When I entered the church, they rang in the New Year.
She has rung the doorbell, but nobody opens.

to ring someone up – *jemanden anrufen*
to ring off – *einhängen (Telefon), Telefongespräch beenden, Hörer auflegen (vgl. hang up)*
to ring someone back – *jemanden zurückrufen (Telefon)*
to ring hollow – *hohl, unglaubwürdig klingen*
to ring the changes on something – *etwas immer wieder auf neue Art versuchen*
to ring for somebody – *nach jemandem läuten*
to ring down the curtain – *den Vorhang niedergehen lassen*
to ring down the curtain on something – *einen Schlussstrich unter etwas ziehen*
to ring out the Old Year – *das alte Jahr ausläuten*
that rings a bell – *das kommt mir bekannt vor, das erinnert mich an etwas*

The terrible voice rang in my ears.
I have already rung for room service to bring us some new towels.
Neil rang the bells.

rise   rose   risen   *aufstehen; (auf)steigen*

On weekdays I have to rise at 6.30 a.m.
Even during the holidays we rose very early in the morning.

The child rose from the floor to shake my hand.
The sun has risen behind the mountain.

Idioms

to rise to the occasion – *sich der Lage gewachsen zeigen*
to rise (up) against someone – *sich erheben gegen, rebellieren gegen jemanden*
to rise from the dead – *von den Toten auferstehen*
Christ is risen! – *Christus ist auferstanden!*
Rise and shine! – *Aufstehen! Raus aus den Federn!*
to rise from the table – *sich vom Tisch erheben*
to rise to the surface – *an die Oberfläche kommen*
to rise to a crescendo – *zu einem Crescendo anschwellen*
to rise in the world – *es zu etwas bringen*
to rise to fame – *berühmt werden*
to rise from nothing – *sich aus dem Nichts emporarbeiten*
to rise above – *ansteigen um mehr als; erhaben sein über*

Übung

I am very worried. His fever has risen by two degrees.
The couple rose from the table.
He rose to fame.

Beachte

> Wie "rise" wird gebildet:
> "arise/arose/arisen" – *sich erheben*
> Man darf "rise" nicht verwechseln mit:
> "raise/raised/raised" – *(er)heben*

run   ran   run   *rennen, laufen*

I run three miles in fifteen minutes.
We ran as fast as we could, but we did not catch the bus.
The thief has run away with the stolen money.

Idioms

to run across someone – *jemandem zufällig begegnen, stoßen auf jemanden*
to run ashore – *auflaufen, stranden*
to run a business – *ein Geschäft führen, betreiben; einen Betrieb leiten*
to run errands – *Besorgungen machen*
to run the household – *den Haushalt führen*
to run the show – *den Laden schmeißen*
to run for President – *für das Präsidentenamt kandieren*
to run out of something – *etwas nicht mehr haben*
to run short of something – *etwas geht einem demnächst aus*

to run someone over – *jemanden überfahren*
to run high – *heftig, hitzig werden (Gefühle)*
to run a temperature – *Fieber haben*
to run dry – *austrocknen*
to run a risk – *ein Risiko eingehen*
to run into debt – *Schulden machen*
to run into trouble – *in Schwierigkeiten geraten*
to run for one's life – *um sein Leben laufen*
to run a race – *an einem Wettrennen teilnehmen*
to run the streets – *sich auf der Straße herumtreiben*
still waters run deep – *stille Wasser sind tief*
it runs in the family – *das liegt in der Familie*

My nose is running. Have you got a handkerchief?   ◄ Übung
He ran his eyes over my dress.
His blood ran cold.
Don't run after every woman in the neighbourhood.
I ran to the bus-stop because I was late.

say   said   said   *sagen*

It is hard to say whether he will win or not.
He said that he was very tired.
What has she just said to you on the phone?

no sooner said than done – *gesagt, getan*   ◄ Idioms
that is easier said than done – *das ist leichter gesagt als getan*
it goes without saying that – *es versteht sich von selbst, dass*
You don't say! – *Sag bloß! Was du nicht sagst!*
You can say that again! – *Das kannst du laut sagen! Das stimmt wirklich, da hast du recht!*
and that's saying something – *und das will was heißen*
that is to say, ... – *das heißt, vielmehr*
let's say – *sagen wir mal*
to say nothing of ... – *ganz zu schweigen von ...*
when all is said and done – *letzten Endes, schließlich, man darf nicht vergessen, dass*
not be able to say boo to a goose – *ängstlich, schüchtern sein*
to say grace – *das Tischgebet sprechen*
to say to oneself – *sich sagen, denken*

Who shall I say? – *Wen darf ich melden?*
Say after me ... – *Sprechen Sie mir nach ...*
There's no saying. – *Das weiß keiner.*
Well, I must say! – *Na, ich muss schon sagen!*
I should say so! – *Das möchte ich doch meinen!*
Well said! – *Ganz richtig!*
Say no more! – *Ich weiß Bescheid!*

Übung ▶

The aborigines of Australia are said to be very friendly people.
Listen, this letter says that they will send you more information.
And then I said to myself: You can't really do that.

see saw seen *sehen*

From our bedroom window we can see the mountains.
I saw them leaving the house.
We saw him talking to her in the garden.
Have you ever seen a kangaroo?

Idioms ▶

not be able to see beyond (the end of) one's nose – *einen engen geistigen Horizont haben, engstirnig sein*
to see no further than one's nose – *engstirnig sein*
to see about something – *sich kümmern um etwas*
to see the back/last of someone – *jemanden loswerden, nicht mehr sehen*
to see for oneself – *sich persönlich von etwas überzeugen*
to see the light – *die Erleuchtung haben, verstehen; zur Einsicht kommen; entstehen, auftreten*
to see how the land lies – *sehen, wie der Hase läuft; die Lage peilen*
to see how the wind blows – *sehen, woher der Wind weht; die Lage abschätzen*
to see someone home – *jemanden nach Hause begleiten*
to see someone off – *jemanden verabschieden*
to see someone out – *jemanden hinausbegleiten*
to have seen better days – *in einem schlechten Zustand sein, schon mal bessere Zeiten gesehen haben*
to see someone's point – *verstehen, was jemand will, meint, denkt*
to see something through – *etwas zu Ende bringen*

to see someone through something – *jemandem beistehen, helfen bei etwas*
to see to it that ... – *dafür sorgen, dass; darauf achten, dass*
to see oneself obliged to – *sich gezwungen sehen zu*
to see red – *rot sehen, wütend werden, in Wut geraten*
to see the sights – *die Sehenswürdigkeiten besichtigen*
to see one's way to doing something – *etwas möglich machen*
not see the wood for the trees – *den Wald vor lauter Bäumen nicht sehen*
Seeing is believing. – *Ich glaube nur, was ich mit eigenen Augen sehe.*
to live to see – *etwas (noch) erleben*

See you later!
See you around!
See you!
Let me see ...
Wait and see ...
I see!

seek   sought   sought   *(auf)suchen; versuchen*

It is too hot in the sun. Let's seek the shade.
We did not know what to do, so we sought his advice.
I have sought to convince her several times.

to seek one's fortune – *sein Glück suchen*
to seek someone's life – *jemandem nach dem Leben trachten*
to seek someone out – *jemanden ausfindig machen; aufs Korn nehmen*
to be much sought-after – *sehr gefragt, begehrt sein*
to seek to do something – *sich bemühen, etwas zu tun*
The reason is not far to seek. – *Der Grund liegt auf der Hand.*
seek time – *Zugriffszeit*
long-sought-for reforms – *lang erstrebte Reformen*

The man went to the library to seek out the information.
The young man sought his fortune.
I'll seek to do it this week, but I can't make any promises.

sell   sold   sold   *verkaufen*

He is trying to sell his old computer because he wants to buy a new one.
My father is a butcher and sells all kinds of meat.
We sold our type-writer to a young lady for 20 pounds.
All the antiques were sold in one day.
Today apples are sold at ten pence each.

Idioms ▶

to sell one's dearly – *sein Leben teuer vekaufen*
to sell someone down the river – *jemanden verraten, betrügen*
to be sold on something – *von etwas überzeugt, begeistert sein*
to be sold – *übers Ohr gehauen werden*
to sell at a loss – *mit Verlust verkaufen*
to sell like hot cakes – *weggehen wie warme Semmeln*
to sell one's soul to somebody – *jemandem seine Seele verschreiben*
to sell oneself – *sich profilieren; sich verkaufen*
to sell somebody on something – *jemanden von etwas überzeugen*
to sell up – *zwangsverkaufen*
The idea didn't sell. – *Die Idee kam nicht an.*

Übung ▶

I am sure his book will sell very well.
I am sorry, but we have no milk left. It is sold out.
The performance was sold out.
They sold their house long time ago and moved to France.

send   sent   sent   *senden, schicken*

Can you sent me your new address, please?
We sent invitations to everybody.
I felt so bad that she sent me to the doctor.
Our friends sent their children to private boarding schools only.
The parcel was sent by airmail.
Anne sent me a postcard from Peru.

to send someone packing – *jemanden verfolgen*
to send someone flying – *jemanden verjagen; zu Boden schleudern*

to send word to someone – *jemandem eine Nachricht schicken*
to send a letter on to – *einen Brief nachschicken (an eine neue Adresse)*
to send somebody to prison – *jemanden ins Gefängnis schicken*
to send somebody to university – *jemanden studieren lassen*
to send prices soaring – *die Preise in die Höhe treiben*
to send shares soaring – *Aktien in die Höhe schnellen lassen*
to send somebody after somebody – *jemandem jemanden nachschicken*
to send away for something – *etwas anfordern*
to send back for reinforcements – *nach Verstärkung schicken*
to send something up in flames – *etwas in Flammen aufgehen lassen*
Send him my love. – *Grüßen Sie ihn von mir.*
she sent to say that ... – *sie ließ ausrichten, dass ...*

My mother sent for a doctor when she saw that I was not feeling better the next day.
I have sent in my application and now I will simply have to wait for an answer.
Mother sends her regards to you.

set set set   *setzen, stellen, legen*

Set the box down on the stairs, please.
I set the book aside when he started talking to me.
We have set up the new washing-machine.

to set someone free – *jemanden freilassen*
to set out for – *aufbrechen, sich aufmachen nach*
to set out on a journey – *eine Reise antreten*
to set out to do something – *sich vornehmen, etwas zu tun; sich an etwas machen*
to set about doing something – *etwas in Angriff nehmen*
to set eyes on something – *etwas zum ersten Mal sehen*
to set fire to something – *etwas anzünden*
to set something on fire – *etwas anzünden*
to set foot in – *eintreten*

to set great store by someone – *große Stücke halten auf*
to set in – *einsetzen, beginnen*
to set one's mind on something – *sich etwas in den Kopf setzen*
to set one's mind at rest – *sich beruhigen*
to be all set for something – *fertig, vorbereitet für etwas sein; bereit, startklar sein*
to set the fashion – *den Ton angeben*
to set the pace – *das Tempo angeben*
to be dead set against something – *entschieden gegen etwas sein*
to set one's face against something – *strikt gegen etwas sein*
to be set on doing something – *entschlossen sein, etwas zu tun*
to set someone a good example – *jemandem ein gutes Beispiel geben*
to set someone's teeth on edge – *jemandem durch Mark und Bein gehen (bes. Geräusch)*
to set a poem to music – *ein Gedicht vertonen*
to set the table – *den Tisch decken (vgl. lay the table)*
to set the alarm-clock – *den Wecker stellen*
to set one's heart on something – *sein Herz an etwas hängen*

Übung

The teachers set us a very difficult task.
You should not have set all your hope on one person.
The film is set in Oklahoma.
The sun sets early in wintertime.
We set him down near the zoo because he wanted to walk home from there.

shake   shook   shaken   *schütteln*

She shakes the rugs every day.
When I asked him whether he had a pen, he shook his head.
The bottle must be shaken before you open it.

Idioms

to shake hands with someone – *jemandem die Hand schütteln*
to shake the dust of a place off one's feet – *eine ungastliche Stätte mit dankbarem Gefühl verlassen*

to shake one's fist at someone – *jemandem mit der Faust drohen*
to shake like a leaf – *wie Espenlaub zittern*
to shake in one's shoes – *nervös sein*
to be shaken by something – *erschüttert über etwas sein*
to shake someone up – *jemanden aufrütteln*
to shake someone's faith – *jemandes Glauben erschüttern*
Shake a leg! – *Mach mal dalli! Tempo! Beeile dich!*
to be shaken to pieces – *durchgeschüttelt werden*
to shake pepper on a steak – *Pfeffer auf ein Steak streuen*
to shake the world – *die Welt erschüttern*
That shook him! – *Da war er platt!*
to shake with cold – *vor Kälte zittern*
to shake with laughter – *sich vor Lachen schütteln*
Shake on it! – *Hand drauf!*
to shake somebody down for 1000 dollars – *jemanden um 1000 Dollar erleichtern*
to shake things up – *Dinge in Bewegung bringen*

My voice shook with emotion when I said that to her.
When there is an earthquake, the earth shakes under us.
I think we have shaken off the police.

shed   shed   shed   *ausgießen, vergießen*

Do not shed tears over it – it is no use anyway.
The soldier shed his blood for his country.
A lot of blood was shed in this terrible war.

to shed light on something – *Licht auf eine Sache werfen; zur Aufklärung von etwas beitragen*
to shed new light on something – *neues Licht werfen auf*
to shed its skin – *sich häuten (Schlange)*
to shed their leaves – *ihre Blätter abwerfen (Bäume)*
to shed its fur – *haaren, Fell abwerfen (Hund)*
to shed a bad habit – *eine schlechte Gewohnheit ablegen*
to shed a few pounds – *ein paar Pfund abnehmen*
to shed one's inhibitions – *seine Hemmungen ablegen*
to shed one's old friends – *seine alten Freunde ablegen*
not shed any tears over someone – *jemandem keine Träne nachweinen*
to shed its load – *Ladung verlieren*
to shed one's blood – *sein Blut vergießen*

Übung

This lamp sheds a very bright light.
The fire in the fire-place shed a pleasant warmth.
You should really shed this bad habit before it is too late.

shine   shone   shone   *scheinen; glänzen*

We usually go for a walk when the moon shines.
Her hair was very beautiful and shone in the sun.
My eyes had shone with happiness before I received the letter.

Idioms

Rise and shine! – *Aufstehen! Raus aus den Federn!*
to shine in/at something – *in/bei etwas glänzen, herausragend sein in einer Sache*
to shine a lamp on something – *eine Lampe richten auf*
to shine a light on something – *etwas beleuchten*
Shine the torch this way! – *Leuchte einmal hierher!*
to shine like a beacon – *wie ein Licht in der Dunkelheit leuchten*

Übung

Suddenly the sun shone out.
Don't shine it in my eyes!
She doesn't exactly shine at mathematics.

Beachte

> In der Bedeutung „polieren" wird "shined" statt "shone" verwendet: He shined the shoes.
> to shine up to someone (AE) – *sich bei jemandem anbiedern*

shoot   shot   shot   *(er)schießen*

Your dog has bitten a child. I am afraid we must shoot it.
Last weekend my father and I shot four ducks.
When he learnt about his company's bankruptcy, he shot himself with a gun.
The policeman was shot by the gangsters.

Idioms

to shoot ahead – *schnelle Fortschritte machen*
to have shot one's bolt – *sein Pulver verschossen haben, keine Argumente mehr haben*
to shoot questions at someone – *jemanden mit Fragen bombardieren*

to shoot the lights – *bei Rot über die Kreuzung fahren*
to shoot a glance at something – *einen schnellen Blick werfen auf etwas*
to shoot a photograph/film – *ein Foto/einen Film machen*
to shoot heroin – *sich Heroin spritzen*
You'll get shot for doing that! – *Das kann dich Kopf und Kragen kosten!*
It was like shooting fish in a barrel. – *Es war ein ungleicher Wettkampf.*
to shoot a line – *aufschneiden; sich wichtig tun*
to shoot the bolt – *den Riegel vorlegen*
to shoot one's bolt – *sein Pulver verschießen*
to shoot dice – *würfeln*
to shoot straight – *genau schießen*
to shoot wide – *danebenschießen*
to shoot for the moon – *sich Großes vornehmen*
to shoot ahead – *an die Spitze vorpreschen*
to shoot by – *vorbeischießen*
to shoot to fame – *auf einen Schlag berühmt werden*
to shoot it out – *sich ein Feuergefecht liefern*
Shoot! – *Schieß los!*
shooting pains – *stechende Schmerzen*

◀ **Übung**

Can you see that rock over there which shoots out into the sea?
He has just shot past me without even saying hello.
Now you've shot your bolt!

show showed shown   *zeigen*

At the border you must show your passport.
You should not always show your feelings.
I showed her my photo-album.
How many times have I shown you how to use the bottle-opener!

◀ **Idioms**

to show someone in – *jemanden hereinführen*
to show someone out – *jemanden hinausführen*
to show off with something – *mit etwas angeben*
to show someone round – *jemanden herumführen*
to show up – *aufkreuzen, erscheinen*
to show one's hand/cards – *seine Karten offen auf den Tisch legen, aufdecken*

to show someone around the town – *jemandem die Stadt zeigen*
to show one's teeth – *die Zähne zeigen*
to show one's face – *sich zeigen*
to show one's gratitude – *sich dankbar zeigen*
to show signs of wear – *Abnutzungserscheinungen aufweisen*
to show somebody to his seat – *jemanden an seinen Platz bringen*
to show somebody round the house – *jemandem das ganze Haus zeigen*
to show through – *durchkommen*
to show oneself – *sich blicken lassen*
to show up badly – *eine schlechte Figur machen*
to show oneself up – *sich blamieren*
Show a leg! – *Raus aus den Federn!*
it only shows when ... – *man sieht es nur, wenn ...; man merkt es nur, wenn ...*
It just goes to show! – *Da sieht man es mal wieder!*
We had nothing to show for it. – *Wir hatten nichts vorzuweisen.*

At the theatre they showed a play by Shakespeare.
I am getting grey hair already. – Don't worry about it. It does not show yet.
She spent very little time on her homework, and it shows!

shrink shrank shrunk *einschrumpfen, einlaufen*

Be careful when you wash your shirt – it may shrink.
My trousers shrank so much in the washing-machine that I cannot wear them anymore.
Look how the sausages have shrunk in the frying-pan!

to shrink (back) from something – *zurückschrecken vor etwas*
to shrink into oneself – *sich in sich selbst zurückziehen*
to shrink away to nothing – *auf ein Nichts zusammenschrumpfen*
to shrink from the truth – *vor der Wahrheit die Augen verschließen*
a shrinking violet – *ein schüchternes Pflänzchen*
shrink-proof – *nicht einlaufend*

The number of participants has shrunk from 1000 to 800.
When his wife died he shrank into himself.
This pullover is shrink-proof.

> Adjektivisch wird manchmal "shrunken" verwendet:
> a shrunken hand, shrunken cheeks – *abgemagert, eingefallen*

shut   shut   shut   *schließen, zumachen*

Now shut your eyes and try to sleep a little!
He shut the door, walked to his seat and sat down.
There is a draught! Please shut the window.
We had just shut the door when she burst into the room.
Stores normally shut at 6.30 in Germany.

Shut up! *(fam)* – *Halt den Mund! Sei still!*
to shut someone up – *jemandem den Mund verbieten, zum Schweigen bringen*
to shut something down – *etwas schließen (z.B. Fabrik)*
to shut something off – *etwas abstellen, abdrehen (z.B. Motor, Maschine, Wasser)*
to be shut off from something – *abgetrennt sein, abgeschlossen sein von etwas*
to shut one's eyes to something – *die Augen vor etwas verschließen*
to keep one's mouth shut – *den Mund halten, schweigen*
to shut oneself in – *sich einschließen in (Zimmer)*
to shut one's mind to something – *sich einer Sache verschließen*
to shut one's fingers in the door – *sich die Finger in der Tür einklemmen*
to keep somebody shut away from something – *jemanden von etwas fern halten*
to shut oneself away – *sich zurückziehen*
to shut oneself off – *sich abkapseln*

There must be something wrong with the window; it simply won't shut.
He shut the book and put it back on the shelf.
The little boy shut his fingers in the door.
The factory was shut down.

sing   sang   sung   *singen*

Nightingales sing beautiful.
Our family sang a few Christmas carols together.
These songs were only sung on very special occasions.
She has been singing in the opera since eight o'clock.

Idioms ▶

to sing another song/tune – *einen anderen Ton anschlagen*
to sing the same song/tune – *ins gleiche Horn tuten*
to sing someone to sleep – *jemanden in den Schlaf singen*
to sing small/low – *klein beigeben, kleinlaut werden*
to sing someone's praises – *Lobeshymnen auf jemanden singen*
to sing out – *laut rufen*
to sing up – *lauter singen (vgl. to speak up)*
to sing something/someone – *etwas/jemanden besingen*
to sing one's heart out – *fröhlich singen*
to sing one's own praises – *sich selber loben*
to sing along – *mitsingen*
They are singing from the same hymn sheet. – *Sie sagen alle das Gleiche.*

Übung ▶

She sang folksongs to me all evening.
He really sung her praises.
She sang her little daughter to sleep.

sink   sank   sunk   *(ver)sinken; (ver)senken*

This ship cannot sink.
I was so tired that I immediately sank into the chair.
The pirates captured the ship and sank it.
Fortunately prices have sunk again.

Idioms ▶

to sink into oblivion – *in Vergessenheit geraten*
to sink into sleep – *in tiefen Schlaf fallen*
to sink into grief – *in Kummer versinken*
sink or swim – *friss Vogel oder stirb; ganz egal, was passiert*
to leave someone to sink or swim – *jemanden seinem Schicksal überlassen*
someone's heart sinks into his boots – *jemandem rutscht das Herz in die Hose*
Now we're sunk! – *Jetzt sind wir geliefert!*

to sink a post in the ground – *einen Pfosten in den Boden einlassen*
to sink money into something – *Geld in etwas stecken*
to be sunk in thought – *in Gedanken versunken sein*
to be sunk in a book – *in ein Buch vertieft sein*
to sink to the bottom – *auf den Grund sinken*
with a sinking heart – *mutlos*
to sink into insignificance – *zur Bedeutungslosigkeit herabsinken*
to sink deeper into recession – *immer tiefer in die Rezession geraten*
to sink away – *abfallen*

◀ Übung

Watch out when you walk on marshy ground! Your feet can easily sink in!
When the soldiers saw the enemies, their hearts sank.
He sank his voice so that the others could not hear him.
The two ships sank immediately after the crash.

sit sat sat — *sitzen*

Why don't you sit down and have a drink?
We did not see very much because we sat here.
I can't go to the cinema because I've got to sit for an exam.

◀ Idioms

to sit back and do nothing – *die Hände in den Schoß legen*
to sit on one's hand – *keinen Finger rühren*
to sit in – *einen Sitzstreik veranstalten*
to sit for an exam – *eine Prüfung machen*
to sit on the fence – *zwischen zwei Stühlen sitzen*
to sit up for someone – *für jemanden aufbleiben, auf jemanden warten*
to sit tight – *ausharren, sich nicht vom Fleck rühren; sich nicht beirren lassen, auf etwas stehen*
to sit up and take notice – *aufhorchen*
to be sitting pretty – *gut dran sein, gut dastehen*
to sit to someone – *jemandem Modell oder Porträt sitzen*
to sit for a painter – *für einen Maler Modell sitzen*
to sit on a committee – *einen Sitz in einem Ausschuss haben*
to sit a horse well – *gut zu Pferde sitzen*
to sit oneself down – *sich gemütlich niederlassen*
to sit around – *herumsitzen*

to take something sitting down – *etwas einfach hinnehmen*
to get sat on – *unterdrückt werden*
to sit a round – *eine Runde aussetzen (Spiel)*
to sit up and beg – *Männchen machen (Hund)*
to sit up to the table – *sich an den Tisch setzen*
Sit up straight! – *Setz dich gerade hin!*
Sit by me! – *Setz dich zu mir!*
He sits for Liverpool. – *Er ist der Abgeordnete für Liverpool.*
The car sits 4 people. – *In dem Auto haben 4 Personen Platz.*

Übung ▶

The clock sat on the desk in front of her.
We sat at the table and waited for my Dad to arrive.
Why do you sit around like that? Come and help me!

sleep   slept   slept   *schlafen*

You look very tired. I guess you sleep to little.
During the holidays we slept out on the beach.
I have slept for half an hour and I feel much better now.

Idioms ▶

to sleep (something) away – *tief schlafen, durchschlafen; etwas verschlafen*
to sleep through something – *etwas verschlafen, nicht mitbekommen, nicht hören (z.B. Wecker)*
to sleep in – *verschlafen, länger schlafen*
to sleep like a log – *wie ein Murmeltier schlafen*
to sleep the sleep of the just – *den Schlaf des Gerechten schlafen*
to sleep on/over a question – *ein Problem überschlafen*
to sleep off one's lunch – *einen Verdauungsschlaf halten*
to sleep it off – *seinen Rausch ausschlafen*
to sleep with someone – *mit jemandem schlafen*
to sleep late – *lange schlafen*
to sleep right round the clock – *rund um die Uhr schlafen*
to sleep around – *mit jedem schlafen*
to sleep out – *im Freien schlafen*
I must sleep on it first. – *Ich muss erst darüber schlafen.*
The house sleeps 20. – *In dem Haus können 20 Leute schlafen.*
let's sleep on it – *schlafen wir erst einmal darüber*

We were so tired that we slept round the clock.
Do you mind sleeping in a sleeping-bag?
Last night the girl slept really well.

slide   slid   slid   *gleiten (lassen)*

My shoes are very slippery – they slide well on the ice.
The ballet dancer slid over the floor.
He has slid his hands into his pockets.

to slide into something – *in etwas hineinschlittern*
to slide out of something – *etwas entgehen*
to let things slide – *etwas schleifen lassen, sich nicht um etwas kümmern, die Dinge laufen lassen*
to slide over something – *über etwas hinweggehen, etwas umgehen (Frage, Thema,...)*
to slide the drawer (back) into place – *die Schublade wieder zuschieben*
to slide down the banisters – *das Treppengeländer runterrutschen*
to slide into bad habits – *(allmählich) in schlechte Gewohnheiten verfallen*
Suddenly it all slid into place. – *Plötzlich passte alles zusammen.*

Nobody saw that he slid out of the room.
The children slid down the hill on plastic bags.
The American dollar is sliding at the moment.

a slide – *Rodelbahn, Rutschbahn; Dia(positiv)*

smell   smelt/smelled   smelt/smelled   *riechen*

I like your new perfume – it smells very good.
The man who was sitting beside me smelt very bad.
I smelt that he had started cooking dinner.
It can be smelt that this is an industrial area.

to smell about/around – *herumschnüffeln*
to smell a rat – *den Braten riechen, Lunte riechen*
to smell fishy – *„faul" sein, nicht stimmen können*
to smell trouble – *Ärger kommen sehen*

to smell of something – *nach etwas riechen*
to smell out – *aufspüren; aufdecken*
That smells! – *Das stinkt!*
His breath smells. – *Er riecht aus dem Mund.*

Übung

Smell this flower! Isn't it wonderful?
I have a very bad cold and I cannot smell.
His coat always smelt of cigarettes.
Wash your hands at once! They smell of fish.
The dog has smelt my hand, but it does not seem to like me.

Beachte

to smell something up (AE) – *etwas verstänkern (Zimmer)*

speak spoke spoken *sprechen*

I must speak to him about this matter soon.
Do you speak English?
My grandfather spoke two foreign languages.

Idioms

Actions speak louder than words. – *Taten zählen mehr als Worte.*
Speak of the devil ... – *Wenn man vom Teufel spricht ...*
not to speak of – *ganz zu schweigen von*
nothing to speak of – *nichts Nennenswertes, nicht der Rede wert*
so to speak – *sozusagen*
to speak one's mind – *offen seine Meinung sagen*
to speak volumes – *Bände sprechen*
to speak well/ill of someone – *gut/schlecht von jemandem sprechen*
not be on speaking terms with someone – *einander böse sein, nicht mehr miteinander sprechen*
English spoken here – *man spricht Englisch*
to speak in a whisper – *flüstern*
Speak, don't shout! – *Nun schreien Sie doch nicht so!*
to speak to oneself – *Selbstgespräche führen*
Speak when you're spoken to! – *Antworte, wenn man mit dir spricht!*
speaking of flowers ... – *da wir gerade von Blumen reden ...; apropos Blumen ...*
to be well spoken of – *große Achtung genießen*

roughly speaking – *grob gesagt*
strictly speaking – *genau genommen*
legally speaking – *rechtlich gesehen*
generally speaking – *im Allgemeinen*
speaking personally ... – *wenn Sie mich fragen ...; was mich betrifft ...*
to speak down to somebody – *jemanden von oben herab behandeln*
to speak in the debate – *in der Debatte das Wort ergreifen*
to ask somebody to speak – *jemandem das Wort erteilen*
to speak for itself – *für sich sprechen*
to speak out in favour of somebody – *für jemanden eintreten*
Speaking! – *Am Apparat!*
James speaking! – *(Hier) James!*
Who is speaking? – *Wer ist am Apparat?*
Speak for yourself! – *Das meinst auch nur du!*

Speak up, please! I cannot hear you.
I am pleased to get to know you. He has spoken of you so much.
At the conference the professor spoke on new methods of curing cancer.

speed   sped/speeded   sped/speeded   *eilen, rasen*

It is great to speed along the beach on a motor-bike.
When he saw his mother coming, he sped down the street.
A racing-car has just sped past our house.

to speed off – *wegrennen, „abdüsen"*
to speed up – *einen Zahn zulegen, beschleunigen*
to be speeding – *zu schnell fahren; Tempolimit überschreiten*
to speed someone on their way – *jemanden vor einer Reise verabschieden*
to speed things along – *die Dinge vorantreiben*
The years sped by. – *Die Jahre vergingen wie im Fluge.*

I could not believe it! Our holidays in the country simply sped by!

We speeded our work up so that we would finish soon.
If you want to see any results, you've got to speed things along a bit.

Beachte ▶

> In der Verwendung "speed up" *(= „beschleunigen")* ist die regelmäßige Form "speeded" üblicher!

spell   spelt/spelled   spelt/spelled   *buchstabieren*

My little daughter can already spell her name.
I spelt my name to the receptionist several times, but she still did not manage to write it correctly.
You have not spelt this correctly. There is an "h" missing.

Idioms ▶

to spell something out – *etwas mühsam entziffern*
to spell something out for someone – *jemandem etwas genau erklären, im Detail darlegen*
it spells disaster – *das bedeutet Unglück*

Übung ▶

Urquhart Castle spells U R Q U H A R T.
I'm sorry, I didn't know your name. That's why I spelt it incorrectly.
Do I really have to spell it out for you?

spend   spent   spent   *verbringen; ausgeben*

She spends every summer with her aunt in New England.
During my stay in Britain I spent most of my time in pubs.
I am afraid I have spent all my money on compact discs.

Idioms ▶

All my energies are spent. – *Alle meine Energien sind aufgebraucht.*
It is money well spent. – *Es ist sinnvoll ausgegebenes Geld, die Ausgabe hat sich gelohnt.*
to be spent up – *abgebrannt sein, kein Geld mehr haben*
time well spent – *sinnvoll genutzte Zeit*
to have spent itself – *sich erschöpft haben; sich gelegt haben*

Übung ▶

I cannot afford to spend more then ten pounds a day.
We spent three hours waiting for them.
He's completely spent up after this holiday.

spill   spilt/spilled   spilt/spilled   *vergießen*

Be careful, do not spill the soup!
The waiter split the red wine all over my new blouse.
I am very sorry but I have spilt some tea on our tablecloth.

to spill the beans – *alles ausplaudern, ein Geheimnis ausplaudern*
to cry over spilt milk – *über Dinge jammern, die nicht zu ändern sind; geschehen ist geschehen*
to spill over with something – *wimmeln von etwas*
to spill out – *herausschwappen; herausrieseln; herausströmen*

It would be terrible if the war spilt over into the neighbouring countries.
Her clothes were spilling out of the cupboard.
The wine spilled all over her new dress.

spin   span/spun   spun   *spinnen; (sich) drehen*

We first have to spin the thread.
The car was hit by a lorry and span across the roadway.
In the past wool was spun with a spinning wheel.

to spin along – *dahinsausen*
to spin away – *wie im Flug vergehen*
to spin a coin – *eine Münze hochwerfen*
to spin a yarn about something/to spin yarns – *Seemannsgarn spinnen, Geschichten erzählen*
to spin out a story – *eine Geschichte in die Länge ziehen, ausdehnen, ausspinnen, weiterspinnen*
to spin out the soup – *die Suppe verdünnen, strecken*
to spin round – *herumwirbeln, herumfahren (sich schnell umdrehen)*
to spin a web of deceit – *ein Lügengewebe spinnen*
to send somebody spinning – *jemanden umwerfen*
my head is spinning – *mir dreht sich alles im Kopf*

Spiders spin spiderwebs.
I got quite a shock when I was driving on the motorway and one of the wheels spun off.
She spun round and hit him in the face.

87

spit spat spat *spucken*

In this country many men spit on the street.
The food tasted so terrible that I spat it out.
He has spat the chewing gum on the street.

Idioms ▶

to be the spitting image of someone – *jemandem wie aus dem Gesicht geschnitten sein, sehr ähnlich sehen*
Spit it out! – *Na sag's schon! Spuck's aus! Heraus mit der Sprache!*
to spit at someone – *jemanden anspucken; jemanden anfauchen*
to spit in someone's eye/face – *jemandem ins Gesicht spucken*
to spit with rain – *Sprühregen, fein regnen*
to spit fire – *Feuer spucken*
to spit something up – *etwas ausbrechen, erbrechen*
She's spitting in the wind. – *Da hat sie sich verrechnet.*

Übung ▶

The cat spat at the dog.
When he was a baby, he always spat out the spinach.
He has spat out a lot of terrible curses.

split split split *spalten*

You can split logs with an axe.
My hair splits easily and has to be cut very often.
My trousers split when I climbed over the fence.
The wood in the backyard needs to be split.

Idioms ▶

to split the difference – *sich auf halbem Wege einigen, sich entgegenkommen über einen Preis*
to split hairs – *Haarspalterei treiben*
to split straws – *sehr pedantisch sein*
to split words – *wortklauberisch sein*
to split one's sides with laughter – *sich vor Lachen schütteln*
to split something off – *etwas abspalten*
to split on someone – *jemanden verpfeifen, verpetzen*
to split over something – *sich wegen einer Sache entzweien*
to split up with someone – *mit jemandem „Schluss machen", eine Beziehung beenden (Ehe, Freundschaft)*

to split something open – *etwas aufbrechen*
to split something into four parts – *etwas in vier Teile teilen*
to split the vote – *die Abstimmung zum Scheitern bringen*
to split at the seams – *aus allen Nähten platzen*
to split on somebody – *jemanden verpfeifen*
I split the seam. – *Die Naht ist aufgeplatzt.*

My head is splitting.
I have split my book up into four different chapters.
If we split the costs between us, it won't be expensive.

spread spread spread   *(sich)ausbreiten, verbreiten*

I spread a blanket over her body.
Epidemics like the cholera very often spread over a whole continent.
He spread the city map out on the table.
Who has spread the news that he has got engaged?

to spread like wildfire – *sich wie ein Lauffeuer verbreiten*
to spread one's wings – *versuchen, auf eigenen Beinen zu stehen; ein neues Leben anfangen*
to spread oneself – *sich viel Mühe machen als Gastgeber, sich sehr anstrengen*
to spread a cloth over something – *ein Tuch über etwas breiten*
to spread the news – *die Neuigkeiten mitteilen, verbreiten*
to spread to something – *etwas erreichen; auf etwas übergreifen (Krankheit)*
under the spreading trees – *unter den ausladenden Bäumen*

The Grand Canyon spread before our eyes.
I spread butter and jam on my toast.
My mother spread out her arms to welcome me.
He spread himself on the comfortable sofa.

spring sprang sprung   *springen*

With my skirt on, I cannot spring over the wall.
When I entered, he sprang up from his chair.
The door had sprung open.

Idioms

to spring to the eyes – *in die Augen springen*
to spring to one's feet – *aufspringen*
to spring to life – *plötzlich kommt Leben in jemanden*
to spring from – *herkommen, herrühren von; abstammen von*
to spring something on someone – *bei jemandem mit einer Neuigkeit herausplatzen, jemandem etwas eröffnen*
to spring up – *plötzlich entstehen, aufkommen*
to spring a leak – *(plötzlich) undicht werden*
to spring a surprise on somebody – *jemanden völlig überraschen*
to spring at somebody – *jemanden anspringen*
to spring open – *aufspringen*
to spring into action – *aktiv werden; in Aktion treten*
to spring to attention – *Haltung annehmen (Militär)*
to spring to arms – *zu den Waffen eilen*
to spring into view – *plötzlich in Sicht kommen*
to spring to mind – *einem einfallen*
to spring to somebody's aid – *jemandem zu Hilfe eilen*
to spring into existence – *(plötzlich oder rasch) entstehen*

Übung

Where did you spring from?
When he saw her at the door he sprang to life.
The island sprang into view as the fog lifted.

Beachte

Im *AE* ist auch die Form "sprung" für Past Tense üblich!

stand   stood   stood   *stehen*

All the seats were occupied, so we had to stand.
He stood on the rock and watched the sea.
We stood up when he entered.
The house stood on the mountain.
Let's go home, I have stood here all day.

Idioms

to stand about/around – *herumstehen*
to stand a good chance of – *eine gute Chance haben zu*
to stand by someone – *zu jemandem stehen, beistehen*
to stand firm – *hart bleiben, unnachgiebig sein*
to stand for something – *stehen für, bedeuten*
to stand in for someone – *jemanden vertreten, für jemanden einspringen*

to stand up for someone – *eintreten für jemanden*
to stand up to someone – *jemandem die Stirn bieten*
to stand up against someone/something – *angehen gegen jemanden/etwas*
to stand someone up – *jemanden sitzen lassen*
to stand on ceremony – *auf Etikette achten*
to stand out from – *herausragen, hervorragen*
to stand pat on one's opinion – *auf seiner Meinung beharren*
to stand together – *zusammenhalten*
to stand the racket – *eine Sache durchstehen; die Folgen tragen müssen*
to stand one's rights – *auf seine Rechte pochen*
to stand someone a drink – *jemandem einen Drink spendieren*
to stand or fall – *siegen oder untergehen*
to stand well with someone – *mit jemandem gutstehen*
to stand something on its head – *eine Sache umdrehen, auf den Kopf stellen*
That stands out a mile – *das sieht ja ein Blinder*
it stands to reason that ... – *es ist ganz logisch, dass ...*
and so it stands – und dabei bleibt es
his hair stands on end – *ihm stehen die Haare zu Berge*

I am afraid we stand alone with our opinion.
Please tell me what you honestly think because I want to know where I stand.
What I admired was that he always stood to his principles.

 Übung

steal stole stolen   *stehlen*

You must not steal!
She went into the shop and stole a bar of chocolate.
I cannot find my wallet; someone must have stolen it.
Last night my bike was stolen.

to steal away – *sich davonstehlen*
to steal someone's thunder – *jemandem die Lorbeeren stehlen, jemandem den Wind aus den Segeln nehmen*
to steal a glance at someone/something – *einen verstohlenen Blick werfen auf*
to steal a march on someone – *jemandem ein Schnippchen schlagen, zuvorkommen*

Idioms

to steal the show from someone – *jemandem die Schau stehlen*
pick and steal – *stehlen, klauen*
to steal somebody's girlfriend – *jemandem die Freundin ausspannen*
to steal the limelight from somebody – *jemandem die Schau stehlen*
to steal up on somebody – *sich an jemanden heranschleichen*

Übung ▶

He is such a mean guy! He has stolen my girl-friend!

stick   stuck   stuck   *stecken; kleben*

Stick the flowers in this jar. I will get a vase for them later.
We tried to stick the broken porcelain figure with glue.
Nails stuck in the wall.
She stuck her head out of the window and shouted "hello" to me.
I have licked the stamp, but it has not stuck on the letter.

Idioms ▶

to stick about – *in der Nähe bleiben, dableiben*
to stick at nothing – *vor nichts zurückschrecken, keine Skrupel haben*
to stick at something – *intensiv weiterarbeiten an etwas*
to stick by someone – *zu jemandem halten, treu bleiben*
to be stuck – *festsitzen, nicht mehr weiter können, stecken bleiben*
to be stuck on someone – *in jemanden vernarrt sein*
to be stuck with someone/something – *jemanden/etwas am Hals haben*
to stick from/out of – *hervorstehen*
to stick something out – *etwas durchhalten, durchstehen*
to stick out like a sore thumb – *auffallen (unangenehm), hervorstechen*
to stick in one's mind – *in jemandes Gedächtnis haften bleiben*
to stick to the point – *bei der Sache bleiben*
to stick to someone like a bur – *an jemanden wie eine Klette hängen*
to stick to one's principles – *seinen Prinzipien treu bleiben*
to stick to the rules – *sich an die Regeln halten*
to stick one's neck out (sl) – *ein Risiko eingehen*

to stick one's nose into something – *seine Nase in eine Sache stecken*
that sticks out a mile – *das sieht ja ein Blinder* (vgl. to stand out a mile)

Simply stick the rubbish in the box.
When I told her to be quiet, she stuck her tongue out at me.
No wonder my tyre was flat! A nail stuck in it.
He has got his hair cut so short that his ears stick out now.

sting   stung   stung   *stechen*

Don't be afraid! Dragonflies do not sting.
In the restaurant the heavy smoke stung in my eyes.
The little girl was stung by a wasp and started to cry.

to be stung with remorse – *von Reue geplagt sein*
to sting someone into something – *jemanden zu etwas bringen; jemandem so zusetzen, dass er etwas tut; jemanden reizen zu; jemanden versetzen in (z.B. Wut)*
to sting somebody into action – *jemanden aktiv werden lassen*
to sting somebody for something – *jemanden bei etwas schröpfen*

Some nettles sting.
She was really stung by his constant insults.

> a stinging remark – *eine bissige, scharfe, verletzende Bemerkung*

stink   stank/stunk   stunk   *stinken*

It stinks in this room – please open a window.
Our house stank of fish because we had had trout for lunch.
After I had eaten at the Greek restaurant, I stank of garlic.
It has never stunk like this in the laboratory before.

to stink of/with money – *vor Geld stinken*
to stink something/someone out – *etwas verstänkern; jemanden ausräuchern*

Something stinks. – *Da „stinkt" etwas, ist etwas nicht in Ordnung, ist etwas faul.*
It stinks in one's nostrils. – *Es ekelt einen an.*
It stinks to high heaven. – *Es stinkt zum Himmel.*
You can stink it a mile off. – *Du kannst es eine Meile gegen den Wind riechen.*
The idea stinks. – *Das ist eine miserable Idee.*
The whole business stinks. – *Die ganze Sache stinkt.*

Übung ▶

His breath stank of alcohol when he came home.
The water stinks of rotten leaves.
The smell of burnt plastic stank us out of the building.

string   strung   strung   *(be)spannen, aufziehen*

He says he will string my guitar for me.
My tennis racket needs to be strung.
I have strung the pearls on a thread.

Idioms ▶

to string someone up – *jemanden aufknüpfen, aufhängen*
to string out along – *in einer Reihe hintereinander fahren (z.B. Autos)*
to string someone along – *jemanden hinhalten (in betrügerischer Absicht)*
to string along with something – *bei etwas mitmachen*
to string together – *aneinander reihen*
to be strung up – *nervös sein*

Übung ▶

I am always strung up before an exam.

strike   struck   struck   *schlagen*

The clock strikes the hour.
The clock struck seven o'clock.
I have been struck on the head by a falling tile.

Idioms ▶

to strike a blow against someone – *jemandem einen Schlag versetzen*
to strike a bargain – *einen Handel abschließen, Vereinbarung treffen*
to strike for/against something – *streiken für/gegen etwas*
to strike a match – *ein Streichholz anzünden*

to strike someone's eye – *jemandem ins Auge fallen*
to strike a root of something – *etwas an der Wurzel treffen*
to strike a happy medium – *zu einem Kompromiss kommen*
to strike while the iron is hot – *das Eisen schmieden, solange es heiß ist*
to strike up a conversation – *ins Gespräch kommen, ein Gespräch anknüpfen*
to strike the right note – *den richtigen Ton treffen*
to strike a false note – *sich im Ton vergreifen; sich daneben benehmen*
to strike it rich – *plötzlich zu Geld kommen, das große Los ziehen*
to strike one's fist on the table – *mit der Faust auf den Tisch hauen*
to strike a blow for something – *eine Lanze für etwas brechen*
to strike one's head against something – *sich den Kopf an etwas stoßen*
to strike the keys – *in die Tasten greifen*
to strike the hour – *die volle Stunde schlagen*
to strike somebody as unlikely – *jemandem unwahrscheinlich vorkommen*
to be struck by something – *von etwas beeindruckt sein*
to strike a light – *Feuer machen*
to strike sparks – *Funken schlagen*
to be struck deaf – *mit Taubheit geschlagen sein*
to strike fear into somebody's heart – *jemanden mit Angst erfüllen*
to come within striking distance – *einer Sache nahe sein*
to strike on a new idea – *eine neue Idee haben*
to strike into the woods – *sich in die Wälder schlagen*
to be struck off – *die Zulassung verlieren*
to strike out for home – *sich auf den Heimweg machen*
to strike on one's own – *eigene Wege gehen*
Does that strike a chord! – *Erinnert dich das an etwas?*
it strikes me that ... – *ich habe den Eindruck, dass ...*
Strike a light! – *Ach du grüne Neune!*

Look at that tree over there! It must have been struck by lightning.
What struck me was that he did not wear a suit that day.
The plan struck me as really stupid.

strive strive striven — *streben*

We all strive for happiness in life.
He strove to become a painter, but he did not succeed.
I have always striven towards amicable agreements.

Idioms

to strive after effects – *Effekte haschen wollen*
to strive to do something – *bestrebt sein etwas zu tun*
to strive with something – *mit etwas ringen*

Übung

If you strive after perfection you will never be content.

swear swore sworn — *schwören*

Before I tell you, you must swear not to say a word about it to your mother.
I swore an oath.
I should not have sworn eternal faithfulness to her.

Idioms

to swear at something – *auf etwas fluchen*
to swear by all one holds dear – *schwören bei allem, was einem heilig ist*
to swear by something – *schwören auf etwas, fest glauben an etwas, von etwas überzeugt sein*
to swear someone in – *jemanden vereidigen*
to swear off something – *einer Sache (Laster) abschwören*
to swear on the bible – *auf die Bibel schwören*
to swear blind that ... – *Stein und Bein schwören, dass ...*
to swear at somebody – *jemanden beschimpfen*

Übung

Our enemies lost the fight and swore revenge.
Does she really have brown eyes? I could have sworn that they were blue.

sweat sweat/sweated sweat/sweated — *schwitzen*

Some people sweat easily in hot weather.
I stayed in bed and sweat(ed) out my cold.
Your shirt is all wet. You must have sweat a lot.

Idioms

to sweat blood over something – *Blut und Wasser schwitzen, sich abrackern für etwas*

to sweat it out – *durchhalten*
to sweat someone – *jemanden schuften lassen, ausbeuten*
to make someone sweat – *jemanden schwitzen lassen*
to sweat like a pig – *wie ein Schwein schwitzen*

I've sweated blood over my exam.

sweep swept swept *fegen, kehren*

My mother sweeps the kitchen floor every day.
A terrible thunderstorm swept the country.
Have you swept the stairs yet?

to sweep across one's mind – *einem in den Sinn kommen*
to sweep something aside – *beiseite schieben, ignorieren (z.B. Argumente, Ratschläge, Einwände)*
to sweep someone off his feet – *jemanden mitreißen, „umhauen", überwältigen*
to sweep something away – *etwas mitreißen, umreißen, fortreißen*
to sweep away someone's doubts – *jemandes Zweifel ausräumen*
to sweep something under the carpet – *etwas zu verbergen suchen, unter den Teppich kehren*
to sweep something off the table – *etwas vom Tisch fegen*
to sweep all before one – *alle in die Tasche stecken*
to sweep the board – *alle Preise gewinnen; abräumen*
to sweep along – *dahinrauschen; entlangrauschen*
to sweep down on somebody – *sich auf jemanden stürzen*
to sweep somebody off his/her feet – *jemanden umwerfen; jemanden begeistern*
to sweep out of a room – *aus einem Zimmer rauschen*
to sweep up after somebody – *hinter jemandem herfegen*
New broom sweeps clean. – *Neue Besen kehren gut.*

Angrily he swept out of the room.

swell swelled swollen *schwellen*

A wasp sting swells up at once.
I have hit my knee and it has swelled up badly.

The day was not so hot that my feet swelled and I had to take my shoes off.
Have you been crying? Your eyes look swollen.

Idioms

Swelled with pride – *stolzgeschwellt*
to swell up with rage – *vor Wut rot anlaufen*

Übung

The sails of the ship swelled out in the wind.

swim swam swum *schwimmen*

You swim a lot faster than I do.
My friends and I swam across the river.
We do not know how long the dead body has swum on the water.

Idioms

to swim the tide/the stream – *mit dem Strom schwimmen, sich der Mehrheit anschließen*
to swim against the tide – *gegen den Strom schwimmen*
to swim in money – *im Geld schwimmen*
to swim before one's eyes – *vor den Augen verschwimmen*

Übung

My head is swimming.

swing swung swung *schwingen*

Tarzan swings from branch to branch like a monkey.
She sat on the swing and swung higher and higher.
He has swung his sword against the enemy.

Idioms

to swing into action – *loslegen*
to swing the lead – *sich vor der Arbeit drücken, krankfeiern*
to swing something – *etwas schon hinkriegen, das Kind schon schaukeln*
to swing round – *sich ruckartig umdrehen*
to swing a child – *ein Kind schaukeln*
to swing one's hips – *sich in den Hüften wiegen*
to swing a door open – *eine Tür aufstoßen*
to swing it (so that ...) – *es so deichseln, dass ...*
no room to swing a cat in – *sehr eng, kein Bewegungsraum*
The club began to swing. – *Im Club kam Stimmung auf.*

He'll swing for it! – *Dafür wird er baumeln!*
He's not worth swinging for. – *Es lohnt sich nicht, sich an ihm die Hände schmutzig zu machen.*

She swung her arms and legs.
Suddenly the door swung open and she came running in.

take   took   taken   *bringen; nehmen*

Why don't you take a sandwich?
We took our dog along to the concert.
I have taken driving-lessons for ten weeks now.
You should not have taken his remark seriously.
We were taken to hospital by an ambulance.

to be taken aback – *überrascht, verblüfft sein*
to be taken with something – *eingenommen sein von etwas*
to take after someone – *nach jemandem geraten, ähnlich sein*
to take a break – *eine Pause machen*
to take something amiss – *etwas übel nehmen*
to take something at face value – *etwas für bare Münze nehmen*
to take a chance – *sein Glück versuchen*
to take a fancy to something – *eine Vorliebe entwickeln für, Gefallen finden an etwas*
to take a liking to something – *etwas ins Herz schließen*
to take something for granted – *etwas als selbstverständlich ansehen, hinnehmen*
to take heart – *sich ein Herz fassen, Mut fassen*
to take something to heart – *sich etwas zu Herzen nehmen*
to take someone in – *jemanden irreführen, betrügen*
to take a look at something – *sich etwas anschauen*
to take to one's heels – *sich aus dem Staub machen, die Beine in die Hand nehmen*
to take notes – *sich Notizen machen, mitschreiben*
to take a notice of something – *etwas beachten*
to take offence at something – *Anstoß nehmen an etwas*
to take place – stattfinden
to take one's leave – *sich verabschieden*
to take one's time – *sich Zeit lassen*
to take someone at his word – *jemanden beim Wort nehmen*

to take someone for someone else – *jemanden mit jemandem verwechseln*
to take effect – *in Kraft treten (Gesetz, Vorschrift)*
to take someone for a ride – *jemanden auf eine Spazierfahrt mitnehmen*
to take someone to ask – *jemandem die Leviten lesen, jemanden zur Rede stellen*
to take to drinking – *zum Trinker werden*
to take turns with someone – *sich mit jemandem abwechseln*
to take the wind out of someone's sails – *jemandem den Wind aus den Segeln nehmen*
Take it from me! – *Das kannst du mir glauben! Das sag ich dir! Verlass dich drauf!*
That takes the biscuit! – *Das übertrifft alles! Jetzt schlägt's aber 13!*
Take it easy! – *Nimm's leicht!*
Take it or leave it! – *Mach, was du willst!*

This is unbelievable! What do you take me for?
The plane took off with delay.
It took a long time to get used to it.
Why don't you take the dog for a walk?

> Wie "take" wird gebildet: overtake/overtook/overtaken – *überholen*

teach taught taught *lehren, unterrichten*

My father teaches at a school for blind children.
My parents taught me not to talk too much.
I was taught to hold the door open for women.
At school we were taught a lot of nonsense.
He has never taught English to adults before.

to teach someone a lesson – *jemandem eine Lektion erteilen (vgl. to learn a lesson)*
to teach oneself something – *sich etwas beibringen*
to teach someone better – *jemanden eines Besseren belehren*
That'll teach him a thing or two! – *Da werden ihm die Augen aufgehen!*
That'll teach you! – *Das wird dir eine Lehre sein!*

My friend taught me to play the piano. ◀ Übung

You can't teach an old dog new tricks. ◀ Beachte
– *Was Hänschen nicht lernt, lernt Hans nimmermehr.*

tear   tore   torn   *(zer)reißen*

Paper tears easily.
She tore several pages out of the book.
When I climbed the fence I tore my trousers.
She tore the letter as soon as she read it.
I was torn between two feelings.

to tear to pieces – *in Stücke reißen* ◀ Idioms
to tear one's hair – *sich die Haare raufen*
to tear something to shreds – *etwas völlig „zerreißen", total niedermachen, vernichtend kritisieren (z.B. Buch)*
to tear a muscle – *sich einen Muskel zerren*
to tear something open – *etwas aufreißen*
That's torn it! – *Das hat alles verdorben!*
a heart torn with remorse – *ein von Reue gequältes Herz*
to be torn between two people – *zwischen zwei Menschen hin und her gerissen sein*
to be completely torn – *innerlich zerrissen sein*
to tear along the dotted line – *an der gestrichelten Linie abtrennen*
to tear past – *vorbeirasen*
to tear away somebody's mask – *jemandem die Maske vom Gesicht reißen*

We tore off our clothes and jumped into the water.
These old houses will be torn down next month.

tell   told   told   *sagen, erzählen*

Tell me about your problems. I will try to help you.
Tell your jokes to somebody else – I do not want to listen to them!
My grandmother tells the most exciting stories.
He told us that his sister had died.
I have told you before that I am not interested in this deal.

Idioms

to tell the world – *etwas hinausposaunen*
to tell someone off – *jemanden ausschimpfen, schelten*
to tell something to someone's face – *jemandem etwas ins Gesicht sagen*
to tell tales – *flunkern*
to tell lies – *lügen*
to tell fortunes – *wahrsagen*
to tell the time by the sun – *die Zeit an der Sonne ablesen*
to tell somebody by something – *jemanden an etwas erkennen*
to tell right from wrong – *Recht und Unrecht unterscheiden*
Who can tell? – *Wer weiß?*
That would be telling! – *Das kann ich nicht verraten!*
it is hard to tell – *es ist schwer zu sagen*
you never can tell – *man kann nie wissen*
You are telling me! – *Du sagst es! Wem sagen Sie das?*
Tell me another! – *Das glaube ich dir nicht! Das glaubst du doch selbst nicht!*
I can tell you that ... – *Ich kann Ihnen versichern, dass ...*
... or so I've been told ... – *... so hat man es mir jedenfalls gesagt ...*

Übung

He never tells the truth. He has told only lies in his entire life.
She always told me to shut up when I was talking too much.
My children are twins. Nobody can tell them apart.
He has never told them about his girl-friend.

think   thought   thought   *denken*

Don't think that I do not like you; I just do not want to go to the dance with you.
We all thought that he was going to die.
Have you ever thought about moving to a foreign country?

Idioms

to think better of something – *einen Entschluss ändern, sich umentscheiden, sich etwas anders überlegen*
to think fit to do something – *etwas für angemessen halten, für richtig halten*
to think something over – *sich etwas überlegen*
to think twice about something – *sich etwas gründlich überlegen*

now that I come to think of it – *wenn ich es mir recht überlege; da fällt mir ein, übrigens*
I thought as much – *das habe ich mir gedacht*
That's what YOU think! – *Denkste!*
to think the world of someone – *große Stücke auf jemanden halten*
to think highly of someone – *eine hohe Meinung von jemandem haben, viel von jemandem halten*
to think something up – *etwas ersinnen, aushecken*
Now let me think! – *Lass mich mal überlegen!*
Just think! – *Stellen Sie sich bloß mal vor!*
I should think so! – *Das will ich aber auch gemeint haben!*
Who do you think you are? – *Wofür hältst du dich eigentlich?*

Do you think he will come? – Yes, I think so.
I should think so!
What was he called again? I cannot think of his name right now.

 Übung

throw threw thrown *werfen*

You can throw the newspaper away now. I have read it.
She threw me the ball and I caught it.
The murderer was thrown into prison.

Idioms

to throw oneself at someone – *sich jemandem an den Hals werfen*
to throw something back at someone – *jemandem etwas vorwerfen*
to throw caution to the winds – *alle Vorsicht in den Wind schlagen*
to throw one's heart into something – *ganz in einer Sache aufgehen, mit Leib und Seele dabei sein*
to throw something in – *etwas einwerfen, einstreuen, hinzufügen (Bemerkung)*
to throw oneself into something – *sich intensiv mit einer Sache beschäftigen*
to throw doubt on something – *Zweifel an etwas aufkommen lassen*
to throw light on something – *Licht auf eine Sache werfen*
to throw cold water on something – *etwas schlecht machen, einer Sache einen Dämpfer aufsetzen*

to throw in the towel – *das Handtuch werfen*
to throw in the sponge – *die Flinte ins Korn werfen*
to throw someone off – *jemanden abschütteln, loswerden*
to throw something over – *etwas über Bord, über den Haufen werfen*
to throw up – *sich übergeben*
to throw one's weight about – *sich aufspielen*
That threw me! – *Das hat mich glatt umgehauen!*

Übung ▶

Within three weeks a bridge was thrown across the river.
I could not understand why he threw his money about like that.
He is a very good rider. His horse has never thrown him.
The burglar threw off the police.

thrust   thrust   thrust   *stoßen*

He usually thrusts you aside and walks through the door ahead of you.
She wanted to kill me and thrust a knife into my chest.
People have thrust themselves forward into the shop.

Idioms ▶

to thrust something down someone's throat – *jemandem etwas eintrichtern*
to thrust home an advantage – *sich eine Gelegenheit zunutze machen*
to thrust one's hands in one's pockets – *die Hände in die Tasche stecken*
to thrust oneself upon somebody – *sich jemandem aufdrängen*
to thrust one's way through the crowd – *sich durch die Menge drängen*
to thrust one's way to the front – *sich nach vorne durchdrängeln*
to thrust oneself forward – *sich vorschieben; sich in den Vordergrund drängen*
to thrust past – *sich vorbeidrängen*

Übung ▶

We thrust our way through the crowd to get to the front.
I was thrust into a dark room and locked up in it.

tread   trod   trod(den)   *treten*

You are not allowed to tread on the lawn.
During the dance he trod on my feet all the time.
People have trodden a path across the meadow.

to tread a dangerous path – *einen gefährlichen Weg einschlagen*
to tread something down – *etwas zertreten, zertrampeln*
to tread on air – *sich wie im siebten Himmel fühlen, in Seligkeit schwimmen, wie auf Wolken schweben*
to tread on someone's heel – *jemandem auf dem Fuß, auf den Fersen folgen*
to tread on someone's toes – *jemandem auf die Zehen treten, jemanden beleidigen, kränken*
to tread softly – *leise auftreten*
to tread carefully – *vorsichtig auftreten; vorsichtig vorgehen*
to tread in somebody's footsteps – *in jemandes Fußstapfen treten*
to tread a fine line between... – *sich vorsichtig zwischen ... bewegen*
to tread water – *Wasser treten; auf der Stelle treten*
to tread the boards – *auf der Bühne stehen*
to tread in – *festtreten*
to tread out – *austreten (Zigarette)*

I trod on a bee and was stung by it.
He trod in his father's foot steps.

Man darf engl. "trod" nicht mit dt. „*trotten*" verwechseln.

undergo   underwent   untergone   *erleben; erdulden*

I pity my friend so much; she has to undergo a terrible cancer treatment.
Our relationship underwent many changes.
We have undergone much suffering in our lives.

to undergo a test – *einen Test bestehen*
to undergo repairs – *in Reparatur sein*

understand understood understood *verstehen*

I do not want you to do that again, understand?
My wife understood children and therefore made a very popular teacher.
Finally I have understood the meaning of the sentence.

Idioms ▶

to understand one another – *sich verstehen*
that is understood – *das versteht sich von selbst*
I understand that ... – *Ich nehme an, dass; ich höre, dass*
What do you understand by this? – *Was verstehen Sie darunter?*
But understand this! – *Aber eins sollte klar sein!*
I quite understand ... – *Ich verstehe schon ...*
so I understand – *es scheint so*

Übung ▶

Although our Spanish war very bad, we managed to make ourselves understood.
This year I have not bought him a birthday present, but I am sure he will understand.

wear wore worn *tragen, anhaben*

Do we have to wear a dinner jacket at the party?
Why do you always wear jeans?
As a child she wore glasses, but now she can see without them.
I have worn a beard for so long that I now want to get rid of it.

Idioms ▶

to wear a seat belt – *einen Sicherheitsgurt tragen, angeschnallt sein*
to wear the breeches/trousers – *die Hosen anhaben, das Heft in der Hand haben*
to wear one's heart on one's sleeve – *das Herz auf der Zunge tragen*
to wear on someone's nerves – *jemandem auf die Nerven gehen*
to wear out – *sich abnutzen, abtragen (z.B. Kleidung)*
to wear someone out – *jemanden ermüden, jemandes Geduld erschöpfen*
to wear out one's welcome – *länger bleiben als man erwünscht ist*

to wear something away – *etwas aushöhlen (Gestein)*
to wear one's years well – *jung aussehen für sein Alter*
to wear white – *in Weiß gehen*
to wear a big smile – *über das ganze Gesicht strahlen*
to wear holes in something – *etwas durchwetzen; etwas durchlaufen*
to wear down – *abnutzen; abtreten; verbrauchen*
to wear to an end – *fadenscheinig werden*
Don't worry, it'll wear off! – *Keine Sorge, das gibt sich!*
as the evening wore on – *im Laufe des Abends*

My mother wears her hair short now.
Your shoes look really worn out.

wear and tear – *Verschleiß*

weave wove woven   *weben, flechten*

It is one of my hobbies to weave carpets.
We wove a wreath and put it on her head.
My jacket is woven from best quality wool.

to weave a plot – *ein Komplott schmieden*
to weave a web of intrigue – *Intrigen aushecken*
to weave one's way through something – *sich durch etwas hindurchschlängeln*
to get weaving on something (be. BE) – *sich ranhalten*

weep wept wept   *weinen*

Do not weep over your fate! You cannot change it.
When he died, she wept her eyes out.
My mother wept for joy when I returned from the trip safely.
Finally she has wept herself to sleep.

to weep for somebody – *um jemanden weinen*
to weep with rage – *aus Wut weinen*
to weep with joy – *aus Freude weinen*

Look at that tree! It is weeping.
She was weeping with joy when she got the news.

win won won   *gewinnen*

I get very annoyed when my brother wins at squash.
Our troops won the battle after only a few hours.
I have won the first prize in the competition.

to win fame – *sich Ruhm erwerben*
to win hands down – *ohne Anstrengung gewinnen, leicht gewinnen*
to win someone's heart/love – *jemandes Herz/Liebe gewinnen*
to win the day/field – *den Sieg davontragen*
to win one's bread – *sein Brot verdienen*
to win someone over to something – *jemanden für etwas gewinnen*
to win something from somebody – *jemandem etwas abgewinnen*
to win free – *sich freikämpfen*
to win through to the finals – *das Finale schaffen*
OK, you win – *OK, du hast Recht; ich gebe auf*

I am sure we will win the election next year.

wind wound wound   *winden; wickeln*

The road winds up the hillside.
The river wound its way to the Pacific Ocean.
This bandage must be wound round your arm.

to wind someone round one's little finger – *jemanden um den kleinen Finger wickeln*
to wind up a clock/watch – *eine Uhr aufziehen*
to wind someone up – *jemanden necken, „aufziehen"*
to be wound up – *erregt, nervös sein*
to wind oneself into someone's affections – *sich bei jemandem einschmeicheln*
to wind up/down the car window – *herauf/herunterkurbeln*
to wind forward/back – *vor/zurückspulen*
to wind one's way – *sich schlängeln*
How does it wind? – *Wie herum zieht man es auf?; Wie herum dreht man?*
to wind itself around something – *sich um etwas schlingen*
to wind up one's affairs – *seine Angelegenheiten abwickeln*

to wind up in hospital – *im Krankenhaus landen*
to wind up with nothing – *am Ende ohne etwas dastehen*

It was very cold outside and she wound a woollen scarf around her neck.

withdraw withdrew withdrawn   *(sich) zurückziehen*

Our troops will have to withdraw.
We withdrew early from the meeting.
The product has been withdrawn from the market.

to withdraw into oneself – *sich in sich selbst zurückziehen*
to withdraw money from the bank/account – *Geld von der Bank abheben*
to withdraw in favour of somebody else – *zugunsten eines anderen zurücktreten*
You can't withdraw now! – *Du kannst jetzt nicht abspringen!*

Later he withdrew his insulting remark.

wring wrang wrung   *(aus)wringen; ringen*

You must wring out the wet shirt before you hang it up.
She wrung her hands in desperation.
His trousers were wringing wet and needed to be wrung out.

to wring someone's neck – *jemandem den Hals umdrehen*
to wring a confession from someone – *jemandem ein Geständnis abringen*
to wring a hand – *kräftig die Hand schütteln*
to wring somebody's heart – *jemandem in der Seele wehtun*

I must go to bed immediately. I am completely wrung out.

write wrote written   *schreiben*

Not everyone can read and write.
A person who writes plays is called a playwright.

109

I wrote her at Christmas, but she has not answered yet.
He has written a book, which he wants to publish.

to write something off – *etwas „abschreiben", vergessen können, nicht mehr benutzen können*
to write shorthand – *stenografieren*
to write someone down as – *jemanden beschreiben als*
to write in for something – *schriftlich anfordern*
to write something up – *etwas auf den neuesten Stand bringen, nachtragen*
to write something to disk – *etwas auf Diskette schreiben*
to write away for something – *etwas anfordern*
That's nothing to write about. – *Das ist nichts besonders; das ist nicht so toll.*
written in water – *in den Wind geschrieben, vergänglich*

Please write back to me as soon as you can.
Can you write down your address for me, please?
I wrote out a cheque for 100 pounds.

Lösungen zu den Übungen

awake:
Seine dumme Bemerkung erregte ihren Zorn. Das Kind erwachte weinend aus einem Alptraum.

be:
Besucher müssen die Ausstellung um fünf Uhr verlassen. Im Moment müssen wir versuchen, ohne seine Hilfe auszukommen. Zieh diesen Mantel nicht an. Er ist altmodisch.

bear:
Ich kann ihn nicht ausstehen. Er ist so ein gemeiner Mensch. Du wirst die Konsequenzen tragen müssen, wenn etwas schief geht. Wir kommen natürlich für alle anfallenden Kosten auf. Mein Misserfolg machte mir lange Zeit schwer zu schaffen.

beat:
Gestern Abend wurden wir von einer Bande von Rowdies zusammengeschlagen. Endlich drängte die Feuerwehr das Feuer zurück. Die Wellen schlugen gegen das Ufer. Was willst du hier? Hau ab!

become:
Wir haben ihn seit Ewigkeiten nicht gesehen. Weißt du, was aus ihm geworden ist.
Was soll aus ihr werden? Bei uns kann sie nicht bleiben.
Ihr neuer Kollege wird zum Problem.

begin:
Wann hast du angefangen, Englisch zu lernen? Er hat vor, nach Alaska zu reisen. Deshalb hat er angefangen, sein ganzes Geld zu sparen. Mein Großvater fing als Fabrikarbeiter an und wurde später Manager. Ich suche ein Wort, das mit X anfängt. Ich hatte gerade angefangen zu lesen, als das Telefon klingelte. Sie fängt den neuen Job nächsten Monat an. Das Kind wurde allmählich müde. Er fängt langsam an zu verstehen. Als das Telefon klingelte, befürchtete ihre Mutter schon das Schlimmste. Der Ärger fing an, als er aus Russland zurückkehrte. Sie versuchte sich zu rächen, indem sie ein Gerücht über ihn in die Welt setzte.

bend:
In diesem Tal macht der Fluss viele Biegungen. Sie bückte sich, um ein Stück Papier aufzuheben. Du solltest dich auf deine Studien konzentrieren. Knick die Seiten deines neuen Buches nicht! Die Stoßstange wurde beim Aufprall verbogen. Ich kann das Bein nicht abknicken.

bet:

Ich wette mit dir um zwanzig Pfund, dass ich dich nächstes Mal im Golf schlage. Alle setzten auf dasselbe Pferd, das leider als letztes durch das Ziel ging. Darauf gehe ich mit dir jede Wette ein. Darauf würde ich nicht wetten. Wollen wir wetten?

bind:

Kannst du mir helfen, sein gebrochenes Bein zu verbinden? Das hätte ich dir gleich sagen können – dieses dumme Vorhaben musste ja schief gehen. Alle unsere Clubmitglieder müssen zum Schweigen verpflichtet werden.

bite:

Der dichte Rauch brannte mir in den Augen. Sein Gesicht sah furchtbar aus – es war schlimm von Mücken zerstochen. Wir sind schon stundenlang hier, aber die Fische wollen einfach nicht anbeißen. Ich mag keine Leute, die an den Nägeln kauen. Hast du von der Katze gehört, die den Hund gebissen hat?

bleed:

Niemand kam ihnen zu Hilfe, und so verbluteten sie. Als er krank war, kam der Arzt und ließ ihn zur Ader. Dieser Mann hat mich völlig ausgenommen. Ich habe kein Geld mehr.

blend:

Meer und Himmel schienen ineinander überzugehen. Sie haben diesen neuen Wolkenkratzer nicht an die Umgebung angepasst. Ich möchte Alkohol nicht mit Milch mischen.

bless:

Alles Gute! Gesundheit! (Wenn jemand niest). Gott schütze Amerika! Du bist wirklich lieb, du bist ein Engel.

blow:

Sie hatte eine starke Erkältung und putzte sich die ganze Zeit die Nase. Das ist ein schönes Foto von dir. Wir sollten es vergrößern lassen. Gott sei dank, der Sturm hat sich endlich gelegt. Es wehte ein starker Wind. Plötzlich flog die Tür auf. Der Wind brachte das Schiff vom Kurs ab. Ihm ist eine Sicherung durchgebrannt. An dem Auto ist ein Reifen geplatzt. Deshalb mussten wir anhalten.

break:

Er brach ihr das Herz, als er sie verließ. Ich bin sicher, dass er nächstes Jahr den Weltrekord brechen wird. An der französischen Grenze brach unser altes Auto zusammen. Als der Krieg ausbrach, verließen wir das Land. Sein Mut verließ ihn, als sie ihn verließ. Er kommt in den Stimmbruch. Wie lange ging die Party gestern Abend?

breed:
Die meisten Vögel bekommen im Frühling Junge. Ich gehe nur mit wohlerzogenen jungen Männern aus. Gewalt ruft nur noch mehr Gewalt hervor.

bring:
Wir müssen die Angelegenheit bald zu Ende bringen. Lass sie aus der Sache draußen. Deine Bemerkung hat ihr die Tränen in die Augen getrieben.

build:
Das ganze Gebäude war aus Holz gebaut. Diese Kamera hat ein eingebautes Blitzlicht. Er ist ein gut gebauter Mann. Er tut nie das, was er sagt, also bau nicht auf ihn. Das Haus befindet sich im Bau. Die Teile bilden zusammen einen kompletten Schrank. Von vielen Knödeln wirst du groß und stark.

burn:
Wutentbrannt verließ er das Büro. Du wirst dich noch kaputtmachen, wenn du zu hart arbeitest. Ich ließ die Kerze abbrennen. Sie bekommt leicht einen Sonnenbrand. Die Säure fraß sich in die Oberfläche. Als sie ihre Schwester erblickte, wurde ihr Gesicht rot vor Scham.

burst:
Bitte erzähl mir davon – ich platze vor Neugierde. Unerwartet platzte meine Mutter ins Zimmer. „Das ist nicht wahr!", platzte sie heraus. Sie brannte darauf, uns das zu sagen. Der Fluss ist über die Ufer getreten.

buy:
Ich habe das Haus einem Freund von mir abgekauft. Die Firma hat alle Verlagshäuser der Stadt aufgekauft. Hast du es geschafft, ihn für dich zu gewinnen?

cast:
Sie hat sich sehr verändert – Sie hat alle ihre Hemmungen abgelegt. Wir werden in der Nähe des Ufers Anker werfen. Gestern hat das Pferd ein Hufeisen verloren. Um seine zukünftige Schwiegermutter zu beeindrucken stellte er sich als Bankdirektor dar.

catch:
Ich fühle mich sehr schlecht, denn ich habe mich schrecklich erkältet. Beeil dich, wir müssen den Zug in fünf Minuten erreichen! Entschuldige, aber ich verstehe nicht ganz, was du gesagt hast. Er hielt das Bild gegen das Licht. Auf den Trick falle ich bestimmt nicht noch einmal herein. Sie blieb mit der Tasche an einem Nagel hängen. Warum schreit er? Er hat sich den Finger in der Tür eingeklemmt. Der Einbrecher wurde auf frischer Tat ertappt.

choose:
Ich entschloss mich, zu Hause zu bleiben, weil das Wetter so schlecht war. Der Politiker wählte seine Worte sorgfältig, als er die Regierung kritisierte. Er wurde zum Sprecher des Ausschusses gewählt.

cling:
Der Gestank von Zigarettenrauch setzte sich in seiner Kleidung fest. Wenn sie übersetzt, klebt sie zu sehr am Text. Es hatte geregnet, und mein nasses Hemd klebte mir am Leibe. Die zwei Frauen halten seit ihrer frühen Kindheit zusammen.

come:
Wir lernten uns im Flugzeug nach London kennen. Eines Tages werden sich meine Träume erfüllen. Beim Lesen des Manuskripts stieß ich auf viele Tippfehler. Warum kommst du nicht mit ins Konzert? Wie kommst du mit deinem Englisch voran? Besuchen Sie mich bald einmal. Er ist weit gekommen. Pass auf! Der Griff hat sich gelockert. Schließlich wurde doch noch alles gut. Ihr Fall wurde vor Gericht gebracht. Sein Bruder ist ganz schön tief gesunken. Das Wasser reichte ihr bis zu den Knien.

cost:
Diese Schuhe kosten ein Vermögen! Ich glaube nicht, dass ich sie mir leisten kann. Seine Vorliebe für schnelle Autos hat ihn sein Leben gekostet. Wie viel kostet die Reparatur?

creep:
Wie hat sich dieser Fehler in deine Arbeit eingeschlichen? Zwei Wochen nach der Scheidung kam er wieder angekrochen. Der Tiger schlich sich an seine Beute heran.

cut:
Es war sehr unhöflich von ihm, sich in das Gespräch einzumischen. Ich habe gerade die interessantesten Artikel aus der Zeitschrift ausgeschnitten. Stein lässt sich nicht so leicht schneiden wie Papier.

deal:
Lasst uns dieses Thema zuerst behandeln. Wir beschränken uns auf die Tatsachen. Sie verhängten Strafen über die Männer.

dig:
Hör auf, mich in die Rippen zu boxen! Sie haben sich einen Tunnel aus dem Gefängnis gegraben. Er musste lange überlegen, um sich an ihren Namen zu erinnern.

dive:
Ich fuhr mit der Hand in die Tasche und zog die Schlüssel heraus. Sie tauchte in der Menge unter. Diese Jungen sind Perlentaucher.

do:
Das ist leichter gesagt als getan. Ich gab mein Bestes, und doch hatte ich keinen Erfolg. Was hast du mit deinen Haaren gemacht? Sie sehen heute so anders aus. Trink das, es wird dir gut tun.

draw:
Wenn das Licht in meinem Zimmer an ist, ziehe ich immer die Vorhänge zu. Man kann das Leben in Afrika nicht mit dem Leben in Europa vergleichen. Welche Schlüsse hast du daraus gezogen? Man muss unterscheiden zwischen meiner persönlichen Meinung und dem, was ich in der Öffentlichkeit sage.

dream:
In meiner Jugend hatte ich viele Träume. Er sah, dass ich alleine nicht damit fertig wurde, aber er dachte nicht im Traum daran, mir zu helfen. Das habe ich nie gesagt! Das musst du geträumt haben! Wer hätte es sich träumen lassen, dass es so kompliziert sein würde.

drink:
Trink deinen Wein aus, wir wollen nach Hause. Wir stießen dreimal auf sein Wohl an. Ich heiratete ihn nicht, weil er ein Trinker war. Darauf trinke ich.

drive:
Schließlich gelang es uns, den Nagel in die Wand zu treiben. Als die Ampel grün wurde, fuhren sie weiter. Ich wurde dazu getrieben.

eat:
Als sie von seinem Erfolg hörte, platzte sie vor Neid. Ich verstehe mich sehr gut mit ihm, denn er frisst mir aus der Hand. Er wird dich schon nicht fressen!

fall:
Die Unterrichtsstunde war so langweilig, dass sie bald einschlief. Sei vorsichtig! Das Buch wird auseinander fallen, wenn du es aufschlägst. Ich habe mich in diese Rolle wirklich hineinversetzt.

feed:
Sie verdiente so wenig Geld, dass sie noch nicht einmal ihre Familie ernähren konnte. Ich gab die Daten in den Computer ein. Die Enten im Park fraßen mir aus der Hand. Die Gefangenen wurden den Löwen zum Fraß vorgeworfen.

feel:
Ich habe immer das Gefühl gehabt, dass mit ihm etwas nicht stimmt. Sagen Sie nur frei heraus, was Sie denken! Er fühlte sich dieser neuen Aufgabe nicht gewachsen.

fight:
Warum hat er nicht zurückgeschlagen, als der Bursche ihn angriff? Meine Eltern stritten sich häufig über dumme Dinge. Er kämpfte um sein Leben.
find:
Ich bin jetzt ein halbes Jahr in New York und kenne mich aus in der Stadt. Schließlich fanden wir eine Lösung für das Problem. Es ärgert mich, dass du nie die Zeit findest, mich anzurufen.
flee:
Weil sie ihn verprügeln wollten, flüchtete sich der kleine Junge zu mir. Er floh, als er den Detektiv erblickte. Das Tier floh vor dem Jäger.
fling:
Sie lief auf ihn zu und warf die Arme um seinen Hals. Die Tür wurde aufgerissen – und herein kam der Direktor. Meine Mutter schlug die Hände über dem Kopf zusammen. Ich glaube, meine neue Hose hat ihr nicht gefallen.
fly:
Es ist windig draußen. Gehen wird den Drachen steigen lassen. Mein Vater flog immer mit Swiss Air. Diese dumme Idee entbehrt jeder Vernunft.
forbid:
In einigen Ländern ist es verboten, in der Öffentlichkeit (Alkohol) zu trinken. Aus Zeitmangel konnten wir nicht näher darauf eingehen. Meine Gesundheit erlaubt es nicht, dass ich nach Frankreich reise.
forecast:
Er konnte die kommenden Ereignisse nicht vorhersehen. Haben sie für morgen Regen vorhergesagt? Es ist nicht immer leicht, eine Wettervorhersage zu treffen.
foresee:
Du hättest diese Schwierigkeiten lange absehen können – jetzt ist es zu spät. Ich kann nicht verstehen, warum die Politiker die Krise nicht vorhergesehen haben. Ich bin sicher, dass er den Unfall nicht vorhergesehen hat.
foretell:
Wer auch immer das vorhergesagt hat – er hatte Unrecht. Niemand kann vorhersagen, was morgen passieren wird. Wenn ich die Zukunft vorhersagen könnte, könnte ich dir einen besseren Rat geben.
forget:
Wie hieß der Film, in dem Robert Redford die Hauptrolle spielt? – Es tut mir Leid, das fällt mir gerade nicht ein. Benimm

dich! Könnt ihr eure Meinungsverschiedenheiten nicht mal ruhen lassen?
forgive:
Sie wird sich das nie verzeihen, wenn den Kindern etwas zustößt. Die Bank wird dir deine Schuld nicht erlassen. Entschuldigung, aber du wolltest doch ins Theater gehen!
freeze:
Im Winter ist der Eriesee oft zugefroren. Ich fror, weil ich meinen Mantel vergessen hatte. Wenn wir Essen übrig haben, können wir es einfrieren.
get:
Ich möchte dich nicht kritisieren – bitte versteh mich nicht falsch. Ich habe das nicht verstanden. Könntest du das bitte noch einmal erklären? Damit wirst du nicht davonkommen!
give:
Nachdem wir vier Tage nach ihm gesucht hatten, gaben wir alle Hoffnung auf. Stell dir vor: Ich habe endlich das Rauchen aufgegeben! Er gab mir sein Wort, es niemandem zu erzählen.
go:
Es tut mir Leid, aber ich muss weg. Mein Auto ist weg; jemand muss es gestohlen haben. Ich kann aus Zeitgründen nicht genauer darauf eingehen. Wenn du das wirklich machen willst, dann tu dein Möglichstes! Macht es dir etwas aus, wenn ich das Radio anmache? – Nur zu!
grind:
Dieses Messer schneidet nicht; es muss geschärft werden. Würdest Du die getrockneten Kräuter bitte fein zermahlen? Der Müller mahlte den ganzen Tag Korn.
grow:
Meine Familie baut Kartoffeln im Garten an. Letztes Jahr ließ ich mir zum ersten Mal die Haare lang wachsen. Wenn ich erwachsen bin, möchte ich Pilot werden.
hang:
Er wurde so ärgerlich, dass er einfach den Hörer auflegte. Er ist durch die Prüfung gefallen. Deswegen hat er sich erhängt. Sie trödeln immer herum, wenn wir spazieren gehen.
have:
Bitte nehmen Sie sich ein Sandwich! Lass mal sehen! Er hatte eine Schwäche für schöne Frauen.
hear:
Ich hoffe, bald von dir zu hören! Es war so leise, dass man eine Stecknadel zu Boden fallen hören konnte. Nein, ich habe noch nie von solch einem Buch gehört. Seit meine Freundin Lucy

nach Australien gegangen ist, habe ich nichts mehr von ihr gehört.
hide:
Ich kann dir alles sagen; ich habe nichts zu verbergen. Heute nachmittag hat mein Hund meine Autoschlüssel versteckt. Sie kann ihre Gefühle nicht verbergen.
hit:
Als sie die Straße überquerte, wurde sie von einem Auto angefahren. Der plötzliche Tod meiner Mutter hat meinen Vater schwer getroffen. Als wir tiefer gruben, stießen wir auf Wasser.
hold:
Sie waren so verliebt, dass sie die ganze Zeit Händchen hielten. Ich hoffe, dass dieses schlechte Wetter nicht lange anhält. Sie glaubt, dass er etwas verheimlicht.
hurt:
Seine Kritik kränkte mich schwer. Der Arzt fragte: Wo tut es weh? Es kann nie schaden, mit jemandem zu reden.
keep:
Bitte behalten Sie Platz! Ich werde es dir erzählen, wenn du ein Geheimnis bewahren kannst. Sie war sehr unzuverlässig, sie hielt nie ihre Versprechen. Betreten des Rasens verboten!
know:
Kannst du Tennis spielen? Er ist als schrecklicher Lügner bekannt. Ich habe sie an der Stimme erkannt.
lay:
Du kannst den Mantel auf meine Couch legen, wenn du möchtest. Er legte eine Falle, um die Maus zu fangen. Glaubst du nicht, du übertreibst ein bisschen?
lead:
Ich frage mich, wo das hinführen soll. Sie brachte mich dazu, zu glauben, dass sie eine berühmte Schauspielerin war. Er führte ein Hundeleben, als er in China war. Ich wusste nie, dass er ein Doppelleben führte.
lean:
Ich lehnte mich vor, um sie sehen zu können. Sie stützt sich auf ihre Ellbogen. Meine Schwester hat sich immer auf ihren Ehemann verlassen.
leap:
Ich erschrak, als der große Hund an mir hochsprang. Das Pferd sprang über die Mauer. Zieh keine voreiligen Schlüsse!
learn:
Ich hab gerade erfahren, dass seine Mutter im Krankenhaus

liegt. Zum Glück hat er aus seinen Fehlern gelernt. Wir müssen dieses Gedicht auswendig lernen.

leave:
Lass das Fenster nachts nicht offen. Unglücklicherweise habe ich sieben Wörter in der Übersetzungsprüfung ausgelassen. Warum überlässt du es nicht dem Zufall? Dann musst du jetzt keine Entscheidung fällen.

lend:
Er fragte mich, ob er mein Fahrrad ausleihen könne, aber ich wollte es ihm nicht leihen. Diese neue Lampe verleiht dem Zimmer eine gemütliche Atmosphäre. Kannst du mir bitte mit dieser Kiste helfen?

let:
Bitte lass mich wissen, wann du ankommst. Ich habe gerade gesehen, dass sie einen Fremden ins Haus gelassen hat. Warum hast du die Tür abgesperrt? Lass mich sofort raus!

lie:
Sei nicht so pessimistisch; das Leben liegt doch noch vor dir. Es tut mir Leid, aber es liegt nicht in meiner Macht, dir zu helfen. Warum liegst du noch im Bett? Musst du nicht in die Arbeit?

light:
Seine Augen leuchteten auf, als er ihre Stimme hörte. Das Zimmer wurde von zehn verschiedenen Lampen erleuchtet. Er hatte Schwierigkeiten, seine Zigarette anzuzünden.

lose:
Wir würden uns in dieser Stadt völlig verlaufen ohne einen Stadtplan. Sie scheint ihr Selbstvertrauen verloren zu haben. Ich habe in den letzten Wochen viel abgenommen.

make:
Hast du die Rede des Präsidenten gehört? Was hältst du davon? Mein neuer Freund hat einen schlechten Eindruck auf meine Mutter gemacht. Ich werde dafür sorgen, dass du auch eine Einladung bekommst. Ihr neues Haus ist aus Holz gebaut.

mean:
Sie waren füreinander bestimmt. Soll dieser Buchstabe ein A oder ein O sein? Hab keine Angst. Er meint es gut.

meet:
Sehr erfreut! Ich hole dich um halb acht vom Bahnhof ab. Gestern habe ich zufällig einen alten Schulfreund getroffen.

pay:
Ich hatte überhaupt kein Geld; ich konnte noch nicht einmal den Zeitungsjungen bezahlen. Es lohnt sich nicht zu stehlen.

Bezahlen Sie bar oder mit Scheck? Ich habe all mein Geld auf mein Konto eingezahlt. Eines Tages werden wir für unsere Sünden bezahlen müssen. Endlich haben meine Eltern das Haus abbezahlt – sie sind jetzt schuldenfrei.

put:
Anders ausgedrückt, ... Ich weiß nicht, wie ich das sagen soll, ... in aller Kürze, ... Wenn Sie sich für diesen Kurs einschreiben wollen, müssen Sie sich in diese Liste eintragen. Wir gehen! Zieh deinen Mantel an und komm mit! In der Jugendherberge wurde das Licht immer um dreiundzwanzig Uhr ausgemacht.

read:
Ich kannte ihn so gut, dass ich seine Gedanken lesen konnte. Er liest die Landkarte, während ich fahre. Ich kann Gitarre spielen, obwohl ich keine Noten lesen kann. Ich kann dieses Buch empfehlen; es liest sich sehr gut.

ride:
Er ritt eilig weg. Wir fuhren mit dem Bus von der Schule nach Hause. Schau ihn an! Er muss vom Teufel geritten sein!

ring:
Die fürchterliche Stimme klang in meinen Ohren. Ich habe schon nach dem Zimmerservice geklingelt, damit er uns frische Handtücher bringt. Neil läutete die Glocken.

rise:
Ich bin sehr besorgt; sein Fieber ist um zwei Grad gestiegen. Das Paar erhob sich vom Tisch. Er ist berühmt geworden.

run:
Meine Nase läuft. Hast du ein Taschentuch? Er ließ seinen Blick über mein Kleid gleiten. Das Blut gefror ihm in den Adern. Lauf nicht jeder Frau in der Gegend nach! Ich bin zur Bushaltestelle gerannt, weil ich spät dran war.

say:
Die Ureinwohner von Australien sollen sehr freundliche Leute sein. Hör mal, in diesem Brief heißt es, dass man dir noch mehr Informationen zusenden wird. Und dann habe ich mir gesagt: Das kannst du nicht einfach so tun.

see:
Bis bald! Tschüss! Auf Wiedersehen! Warte mal/mal sehen sehen/mal überlegen ... Kommt Zeit, kommt Rat; abwarten und Tee trinken. Ah, ich verstehe!

seek:
Der Mann ging in die Bibliothek, um die Informationen herauszusuchen. Der junge Mann suchte sein Glück. Ich werde

mich bemühen, es diese Woche zu erledigen, aber ich kann nichts versprechen.

sell:
Ich bin sicher, dass dieses Buch gut gehen wird. Es tut mir Leid, aber wir haben keine Milch mehr; sie ist ausverkauft. Wir bekamen keine Karten, weil das Theater ausverkauft war. Die Vorstellung war ausverkauft. Sie haben ihr Haus schon vor langer Zeit verkauft und sind nach Frankreich gezogen.

send:
Meine Mutter ließ einen Arzt kommen, als sie sah, dass ich mich am nächsten Tag nicht besser fühlte. Ich habe meine Bewerbung eingeschickt, und jetzt werde ich einfach abwarten müssen. Mutter lässt dich grüßen.

set:
Die Lehrer stellten uns eine sehr schwierige Aufgabe. Du hättest nicht all deine Hoffnung auf eine Person setzen sollen. Der Film spielt in Oklahoma. Die Sonne geht im Winter früh unter. Wir ließen ihn in der Nähe des Zoos aussteigen, weil er von dort aus zu Fuß heimgehen wollte.

shake:
Meine Stimme zitterte vor Erregung, als ich das zu ihr sagte. Bei einem Erdbeben bebt die Erde unter uns. Ich glaube, wir haben die Polizei abgeschüttelt.

shed:
Diese Lampe verbreitet ein sehr helles Licht. Das Feuer im Kamin verbreitete eine angenehme Wärme. Du solltest diese schlechte Angewohnheit wirklich ablegen, bevor es zu spät ist.

shine:
Plötzlich schien die Sonne hervor. Blende mich nicht! Sie ist nicht gerade eine Leuchte in Mathematik.

shoot:
Kannst du den Felsen da drüben sehen, der ins Meer hinausragt? Er ist gerade an mit vorbeigeschossen, ohne auch nur zu grüßen. Jetzt hast du dein Pulver verschossen.

show:
Im Theater zeigten sie ein Shakespearestück. Ich bekomme schon graue Haare. – Mach dir keine Sorgen – man sieht es noch nicht. Sie hat sehr wenig Zeit auf Ihre Hausaufgaben verwendet, und das sieht man!

shrink:
Die Teilnehmerzahl ist von 1000 auf 800 gesunken. Als seine Frau starb, zog er sich in sich selbst zurück. Dieser Pullover geht nicht ein.

shut:
Da stimmt etwas nicht mit dem Fenster; es lässt sich einfach nicht schließen. Er schloss das Buch und stellte es zurück ins Regal. Der kleine Junge klemmte sich die Finger in der Tür ein. Die Fabrik wurde geschlossen.
sing:
Sie sang mir den ganzen Abend Volkslieder vor. Er hat wirklich Lobeshymnen auf sie gesungen. Sie sang ihre kleine Tochter in den Schlaf.
sink:
Pass auf, wenn du über sumpfigen Boden gehst; deine Füße können leicht einsinken. Als die Soldaten die Feinde sahen, verließ sie der Mut. Er senkte seine Stimme, sodass die anderen ihn nicht hören konnten. Die zwei Schiffe sanken sofort nach dem Zusammenstoß.
sit:
Die Uhr stand vor ihr auf dem Tisch. Wir saßen am Tisch und warteten auf die Ankunft meines Vaters. Warum sitzt du so herum? Komm und hilf mir!
sleep:
Wir waren so müde, dass wir vierundzwanzig Stunden durchschliefen. Macht es dir etwas aus, im Schlafsack zu schlafen? Vergangene Nacht schlief das Mädchen wirklich wunderbar.
slide:
Niemand sah, dass er aus dem Zimmer schlüpfte. Die Kinder rutschten auf Plastiktüten den Hügel hinunter. Der amerikanische Dollar fällt im Moment.
smell:
Riech mal an dieser Blume! Ist sie nicht wunderbar? Ich habe eine sehr starke Erkältung und kann nichts riechen. Sein Mantel roch immer nach Zigaretten. Wasch dir sofort die Hände! Sie riechen nach Fisch. Der Hund hat an meiner Hand geschnuppert, scheint mich aber nicht zu mögen.
speak:
Sprechen Sie bitte lauter! Ich kann Sie nicht hören. Ich freue mich, Sie kennen zu lernen. Er hat so viel von Ihnen gesprochen. Auf der Konferenz hielt der Professor einen Vortrag über neue Methoden der Krebsheilung.
speed:
Ich konnte es kaum glauben – unsere Ferien auf dem Lande vergingen wie im Flug. Wir beschleunigten unsere Arbeit, damit wir bald fertig würden. Wenn du Ergebnisse sehen willst, musst du die Dinge ein wenig vorantreiben.

spell:
Urquhart Castle schreibt sich U R Q U H A R T. Es tut mir Leid, ich wusste deinen Namen nicht. Deshalb habe ich ihn falsch geschrieben. Muss ich dir das wirklich bis ins Detail erklären?
spend:
Ich kann mir nicht leisten, mehr als zehn Pfund am Tag auszugeben. Wir warteten drei Stunden auf sie. Nach diesem Urlaub ist er völlig abgebrannt.
spill:
Es wäre furchtbar, wenn der Krieg sich auf die Nachbarländer ausbreiten würde. Ihre Kleidungsstücke quollen aus dem Schrank. Der Wein war über ihr ganzes neues Kleid verschüttet.
spin:
Spinnen spinnen Spinnweben. Ich bekam einen ziemlichen Schock, als ich auf der Autobahn fuhr und sich ein Rad abdrehte. Sie wirbelte herum und schlug ihn ins Gesicht.
spit:
Die Katze fauchte den Hund an. Als Baby spuckte er immer den Spinat aus. Er hat viele schreckliche Flüche ausgestoßen.
split:
Ich habe fürchterliche Kopfschmerzen. Ich habe mein Buch in vier verschiedene Kapitel aufgeteilt. Wenn wir uns die Kosten teilen, ist es nicht teuer.
spread:
Der Grand Canyon erstreckte sich vor unseren Augen. Ich strich Butter und Marmelade auf mein Toast. Meine Mutter breitete die Arme zur Begrüßung aus. Er streckte sich auf dem bequemen Sofa aus.
spring:
Wo kommst du denn plötzlich her? Als er sie an der Türe sah, kam plötzlich Leben in ihn. Die Insel kam plötzlich in Sicht, als sich der Nebel lichtete.
stand:
Ich fürchte, wir stehen mit unserer Meinung alleine da. Bitte sage mir ehrlich, was du denkst, weil ich wissen möchte, woran ich bin. Was ich bewunderte, war, dass er immer zu seinen Prinzipien stand.
steal:
Er ist so ein gemeiner Kerl; er hat mir meine Freundin ausgespannt.
stick:
Steck den Müll einfach in die Kiste. Als ich ihr sagte, sie solle ruhig sein, streckte sie mir die Zunge heraus. Kein Wunder,

dass mein Reifen platt war! Es steckte ein Nagel darin! Er hat sich die Haare so kurz schneiden lassen, dass jetzt seine Ohren abstehen.

sting:
Einige Nesseln brennen. Sie war wirklich gekränkt über seine ständigen Beleidigungen.

stink:
Sein Atem stank nach Alkohol, als er heimkam. Das Wasser stinkt nach verfaulten Blättern. Der Gestank von verbranntem Plastik vertrieb uns aus dem Gebäude.

string:
Ich bin immer angespannt vor einer Prüfung.

strike:
Schau dir mal den Baum da drüben an; da hat wohl der Blitz eingeschlagen. Was mir auffiel, war, dass er an jenem Tag keinen Anzug trug. Der Plan kam mir wirklich blöd vor.

strive:
Wenn du nach Perfektion strebst, wirst du nie zufrieden sein.

swear:
Unsere Feinde verloren den Kampf und schworen Rache. Hat sie wirklich braune Augen? Ich hätte schwören können, dass sie blau waren.

sweat:
Für mein Examen habe ich mich abgerackert.

sweep:
Ärgerlich rauschte er aus dem Zimmer.

swell:
Die Segel des Schiffes blähten sich im Wind.

swim:
In meinem Kopf dreht sich alles.

swing:
Sie schlenkerte mit den Armen und baumelte mit den Beinen. Plötzlich flog die Tür auf und sie kam hereingerannt.

take:
Das ist unglaublich! Wofür halten Sie mich denn? Das Flugzeug startete mit Verspätung. Es dauerte lange, sich daran zu gewöhnen. Warum gehst du nicht mit dem Hund spazieren? Letzte Woche trat das neue Gesetz in Kraft.

teach:
Mein Freund brachte mir Klavierspielen bei.

tear:
Wir rissen uns die Kleider vom Leib und sprangen ins Wasser. Diese alten Häuser werden nächsten Monat abgerissen.

tell:
Er sagt nie die Wahrheit; er hat in seinem ganzen Leben nur Lügen erzählt. Sie befahl mir immer, den Mund zu halten, wenn ich zu viel redete. Meine Kinder sind Zwillinge; niemand kann sie auseinander halten. Er hat ihnen nie von seiner Freundin erzählt.

think:
Glaubst du, dass er kommen wird? – Ja, ich glaube schon. Ich denke doch/das will ich meinen! Wie hieß er noch mal? Sein Name fällt mir im Moment nicht ein.

throw:
Innerhalb von drei Wochen hatte man eine Brücke über den Fluss geschlagen. Ich konnte nicht verstehen, warum er so mit seinem Geld um sich warf. Er ist ein sehr guter Reiter; sein Pferd hat ihn noch nie abgeworfen. Der Einbrecher schüttelte die Polizei ab.

thrust:
Wir schoben uns durch die Menge, um nach vorne zu gelangen. Ich wurde in einen dunklen Raum gestoßen und darin eingesperrt.

tread:
Ich trat auf eine Biene und wurde von ihr gestochen. Er trat in die Fußstapfen seines Vaters.

understand:
Obwohl wir sehr schlecht Spanisch konnten, gelang es uns, uns verständlich zu machen. Ich habe ihm dieses Jahr kein Geburtstagsgeschenk gekauft, aber ich bin sicher, er wird Verständnis dafür haben.

wear:
Meine Mutter trägt jetzt die Haare kurz. Deine Schuhe sehen richtig abgetragen aus.

weep:
Schau mal der Baum da! Er lässt die Zweige hängen. Sie weinte vor Freude, als sie die Nachricht bekam.

win:
Ich bin sicher, dass wir nächstes Jahr die Wahl gewinnen.

wind:
Es war sehr kalt draußen, und sie wickelte sich einen Wollschal um den Hals.

withdraw:
Später zog er seine beleidigende Bemerkung zurück.

wring:
Ich muss sofort ins Bett. Ich bin völlig fertig.

write:
Bitte schreib so bald wie möglich zurück. Kannst du mir bitte deine Adresse aufschreiben? Ich schrieb einen Scheck über hundert Pfund aus.

Anhang

abide	abode/abided	abode/abided	*bleiben; wohnen*
befall	befell	befallen	*widerfahren*
beget	begot	begotten	*(er)zeugen*
behold	beheld	beheld	*erblicken*
beset	beset	beset	*ersetzen, einschließen*
bid	bade/bid	bidden/bid	*gebieten, lassen*
broadcast	broadcast/ed	broadcast/ed	*durch Rundfunk senden*
browbeat	browbeat	browbeaten	*tyrannisieren*
chide	chid	chidden, chid	*schelten*
cleave	clove/cleft	cloven/cleft	*spalten*
forbear	forbore	forborne	*sich enthalten*
forsake	forsook	forsaken	*aufgeben*
gild	gilded/gilt	gilded/gilt	*vergolden*
heave	heaved/hove	heaved/hove	*heben, hieven*
hew	hewed	hewed/hewn	*hauen, hacken*
kneel	knelt	knelt	*knien*
knit	knitted/knit	knitted/knit	*stricken*
lade	laded	laden	*laden*
melt	melted	melted/molten	*schmelzen*
mistake	mistook	mistaken	*verwechseln*
mow	mowed	mowed	*mähen*
overbear	overbore	overborne	*überwältigen*
overcome	overcame	overcome	*überwältigen*
partake	partook	partaken	*teilnehmen*
rend	rent	rent	*zerreißen*
rid	rid	rid	*befreien*
rive	rived	rived/riven	*(sich) spalten*
shear	sheared	sheared/shorn	*scheren*
shoe	shod	shod	*beschuhen, schlagen*
slay	slew	slain	*erschlagen*
sling	slung	slung	*schleudern*
slink	slunk	slunk	*schleichen*
smite	smote	smitten	*treffen, schlagen*
sow	sowed	sown	*säen*
spoil	spoilt/spoiled	spoilt/spoiled	*verderben*
strew	strewed	strewn	*streuen*
stride	strode	stridden	*schreiten*
thrive	throve	thriven	*gedeihen*
upset	upset	upset	*umwerfen; beunruhigen*
withhold	withheld	withheld	*zurückhalten*
withstand	withstood	withstood	*widerstehen*
work	wrought	wrought	*bewirken*